Folk-Art Favorites

Quilts from Joined at the Hip

Martingale®

Folk-Art Favorites: Quilts from Joined at the Hip
© 2009 by Tammy Johnson and Avis Shirer

That Patchwork Place® is an imprint
of Martingale & Company®.

Martingale & Company
20205 144th Ave. NE
Woodinville, WA 98072-8478 USA
www.martingale-pub.com

Printed in China
14 13 12 11 10 09   8 7 6 5 4 3 2 1

**Library of Congress
Cataloging-in-Publication Data**
Library of Congress Control Number: 2009003175
ISBN: 978-1-56477-884-0

ᴌ/120   4560 9/09

Mission Statement

*Dedicated to providing quality products
and service to inspire creativity.*

Credits

President & CEO: Tom Wierzbicki

Editor in Chief: Mary V. Green

Managing Editor: Tina Cook

Technical Editor: Laurie Baker

Copy Editor: Sheila Chapman Ryan

Design Director: Stan Green

Production Manager: Regina Girard

Illustrator: Laurel Strand

Cover & Text Designer: Regina Girard

Photographer: Brent Kane

Contents

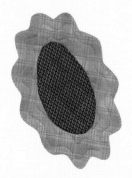

Introduction

Folk art is defined as "the traditional, typically anonymous art of usually untrained people" *(Merriam-Webster's 11th Collegiate Dictionary)*. That definition does describe the projects in this book. Tammy and I have no formal art training. We certainly know that pineapples should not be the same size as a house, but we like that look. We can't explain it, but we are drawn to objects that are out of proportion, whimsical, and offbeat. Like someone once said about riding motorcycles, "If you have to ask, you'll never understand." That phrase says it so well. Folk art is the same; you see it and immediately, you're hooked.

Enjoy the projects within this book.

~Avis

Appliqué and Quiltmaking Basics

The techniques we use to make our quilts include basic rotary cutting, some shortcut piecing, and fusible appliqué that we like to finish with machine blanket stitching for a decorative touch. You may be familiar with all of these techniques already, but if you need some guidance, we've covered the basics for you in this section.

Supplies

Rotary-cutting tools. You'll need a cutting mat, rotary cutter, and clear acrylic rulers to complete the projects in this book. Rulers come in many shapes and sizes. A 6" x 24" long ruler and a 12½" square ruler are good sizes to start with.

Sewing machine. A sewing machine in good working order is a must-have. The majority of stitching is done with a straight stitch. We use a machine blanket stitch to finish the edges of fused appliqué shapes. If you plan to machine quilt your projects as we've done, you will find a walking foot and a darning foot very helpful.

Fusible web. If you want to stitch around the edges of the fused appliqués, make sure to use a lightweight fusible web.

Batting. While there are many types of batting available, we used cotton batting for all of the quilts in this book. Cotton batting gives a very flat look, and if the finished quilt is washed, it will take on the look of a crinkled antique quilt.

Rotary Cutting

Rotary cutting will make the process of constructing a quilt more accurate and much faster than cutting the pieces with scissors. The following steps will guide you in the process.

(1) Fold the fabric with the selvages together. Lay the fabric on the cutting mat with the fold toward you, aligning the fabric on a horizontal line on the mat.

(2) Lay a small square ruler along the folded edge of the fabric, aligning a line on the ruler with the folded edge of the fabric. Then lay a long ruler to the left of the square ruler so that the edges touch.

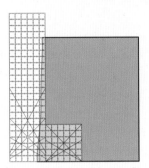

(3) Remove the square ruler, keeping the long ruler in place. Cut along the right edge of the long ruler with a rotary cutter. The edge of the fabric is now straight and ready for you to cut your strips.

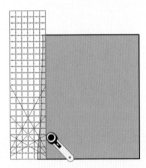

(4) Line up the straight edge of the fabric with the line on the ruler that corresponds with the required measurement. Cut the strip.

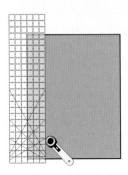

(5) To crosscut the strip, trim the selvages off the ends of the strip. Line up the left side of the strip with the correct ruler line. Cut along the right edge of the ruler.

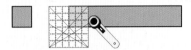

(6) To cut a half-square triangle, cut a square the size indicated in the cutting instructions. Lay a ruler across the square diagonally and cut from corner to corner. One square will yield two half-square triangles.

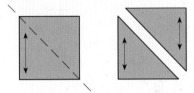

Folded Corners

One piecing shortcut we use often to make some of the blocks in our quilts is the folded-corner technique. It makes quick work of adding diagonal corners to squares and rectangles and gives neat and accurate results. The block instructions will give the sizes to cut each piece. The following steps explain how to do the piecing.

(1) Fold the square that will be used to make the corner in half diagonally and crease it to mark the stitching line. Or, use a pencil and ruler to draw a diagonal line from corner to corner on the wrong side of the square.

Crease or pencil line

(2) Place the square right sides together with the strip, rectangle, or larger square as shown in the project illustration. Make sure the diagonal line is pointing in the correct direction, and then stitch on the creased or drawn stitching line.

Stitch.

③ Trim away the outer corner of the square, cutting ¼" from the stitching line. Leave the bottom layer (square, rectangle, or strip) intact. This will help stabilize the corner. Flip open the top square of fabric and press to complete the folded corner.

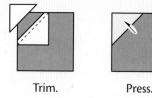

Trim.   Press.

Fusible Appliqué

We generally use fusible appliqué because it's fast and easy, making this collection of quilts a snap to complete. For this technique, the patterns need to be reversed from the image shown in the completed quilt. In this book, we've already reversed the patterns for you.

① Trace the pattern onto the paper side of the fusible-web material.

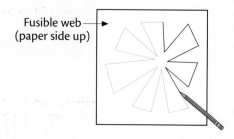

Fusible web (paper side up)

② Cut out the shape, cutting about ¼" *outside* of the traced line. Do not cut on the line!

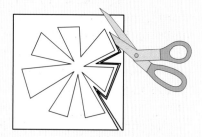

③ Place the fusible-web shape, traced side up, on the wrong side of the appropriate fabric. Use your iron to press the fusible web onto the fabric following the manufacturer's instructions.

Cut out the shape along the traced line. Remove the paper backing.

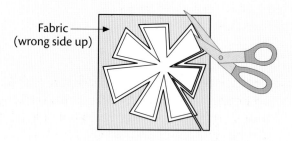

Fabric (wrong side up)

④ Place the appliqué shape with the shiny adhesive side down on the right side of the background fabric and press in place.

⑤ Finish the edges of the appliqués by stitching around them with a decorative stitch and matching thread. We used a machine blanket stitch for most of the appliqués in this book.

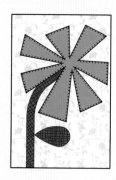

Making and Applying Bias Stems

We've used bias strips to make the stem appliqués in some of the projects in this book. Refer to the specific project instructions for the dimensions of the strips. Make the strips as follows.

① Use a rotary cutter, a mat, and an acrylic ruler to cut a strip of vine fabric *on the bias.* Trim the strip to the length specified if necessary.

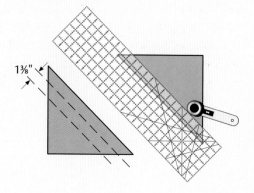

1⅜"

② Press under ¼" on both long edges of the strip.

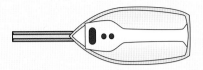

③ Position the strip on the background fabric according to the project instructions and stitch it in place by machine using a blind hem stitch. We use a thread color that blends well with the background fabric. You will need to adjust the stitch length and width to a very short and narrow stitch. Stitch close to the edge of the strip, stitching on the background fabric. The machine will stitch about five straight stitches and then jump over to catch the edge of the appliqué. You may want to practice on a fabric scrap first. The result is nearly invisible, imitating the look of hand appliqué.

Quilting and Binding

When the quilt top is done, make a "sandwich" by layering the backing fabric, batting, and quilt top. The batting and backing pieces are cut 6" larger all around than the quilt top.

① Lay the backing fabric face down on a flat surface. Secure the edges with masking tape to keep the backing smooth but not stretched.

② Lay the batting piece on top of the backing. Smooth out all the wrinkles, and then center the quilt top face up over the batting.

③ Baste the sandwich using a needle and thread, safety pins, or basting spray.

④ Quilt as desired by hand or machine. The quilts in this book were machine quilted.

⑤ We like to use single-fold binding to finish the quilt edges. Cut 1½"-wide strips across the width of the binding fabric to make single-fold binding. Join the strips to make one strip long enough to go all the way around the quilt plus at least 10" for turning the corners and finishing the ends.

⑥ Stitch the binding in place on the right side of the quilt top through all the layers, raw edges aligned, using a ¼" seam allowance. Start at the middle of the lower edge of the quilt. Start stitching 1" from the end of the binding strip. Stop stitching ¼" from the corner of the quilt. Backstitch and cut the thread. Turn the quilt so you can sew down the next side. Fold the binding strip up, forming a 45° angle. Bring the binding strip down on itself. Stitch along the edge, again using a ¼" seam allowance.

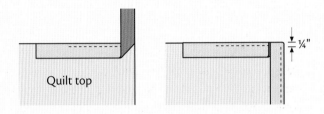

⑦ Repeat this process for each corner. When you are close to the beginning of the binding, fold back the 1" tail that was left at the start of the binding. Then overlap the other end of the binding with the 1" folded edge and continue stitching to hold all three layers in place. Trim away any excess binding.

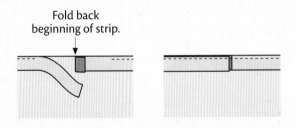

⑧ Using a long ruler and rotary cutter, trim the batting and backing even with the edge of the quilt top. Fold the binding over the raw edge of the quilt. Hand stitch the binding in place using a blind stitch, turning under ¼" on the raw edge of the binding strip as you go.

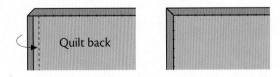

Pomegranate Christmas

The pomegranate pattern has always been a favorite of mine.
The rich golds and reds in this quilt make it perfect for Christmas.

~Avis

Materials

Yardage is based on 42"-wide fabric.

4 yards *total* of assorted beige fabrics for appliqué block backgrounds

⅜ yard *each* of 8 assorted gold fabrics for pieced blocks

⅜ yard *each* of 8 assorted red fabrics for pieced blocks

1⅝ yards of red striped fabric for outer border

1½ yards of green print 1 for lower leaf appliqués

1⅜ yards of red print for outer bud appliqués

1⅓ yards of taupe print for upper leaf appliqués

1 yard of gold print for middle bud appliqués and inner border

⅜ yard of green print 2 for stem appliqués

⅓ yard of red-and-gold print for inner bud appliqués

½ yard of red checked fabric for binding

8½ yards of fabric for backing

98" x 108" piece of batting

10 yards of paper-backed fusible web

Cutting

The appliqué patterns are found on page 17. For more information on cutting pieces for fusible appliqué, refer to "Fusible Appliqué" on page 6.

From *each* of the 8 assorted gold fabrics, cut:
• 4 strips, 2½" x 42"; crosscut into 60 squares, 2½" x 2½" (480 total)

From *each* of the 8 assorted red fabrics, cut:
• 4 strips, 2½" x 42"; crosscut into 60 squares, 2½" x 2½" (480 total)

From the assorted beige fabrics, cut a *total* of:
• 60 squares, 8½" x 8½"

From the gold print, cut:
• 9 strips, 1½" x 42"
• 60 middle bud appliqué shapes

From the green print 1, cut:
• 60 lower leaf appliqué shapes

From the green print 2, cut:
• 60 stem appliqué shapes

From the taupe print, cut:
• 60 upper leaf appliqué shapes

From the red print, cut:
• 60 outer bud appliqué shapes

From the red-and-gold print, cut:
• 60 inner bud appliqué shapes

From the red striped fabric, cut:
• 9 strips, 5½" x 42"

From the red checked fabric, cut:
• 10 strips, 1½" x 42"

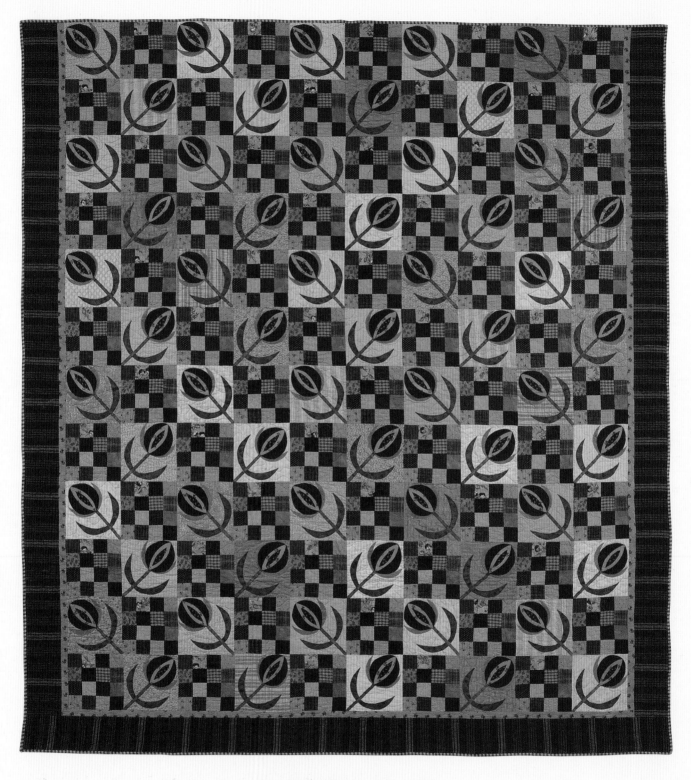

Finished quilt size: 92" x 102"

Finished block size: 8" x 8"

Constructing the Pieced Blocks

Stitch eight assorted gold 2½" squares and eight assorted red 2½" squares together as shown. Repeat to make a total of 60 blocks.

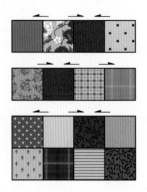

Make 60.

Constructing the Appliquéd Blocks

Refer to "Fusible Appliqué" on page 6 and the photo on page 10 to position one of each of the appliqué shapes on a beige 8½" background square. The end of the stem should be placed in the corner of the background square. When you are happy with the placement, fuse the shapes in place. Machine blanket stitch around each appliqué shape with matching thread. Repeat to make a total of 60 blocks.

Make 60.

Assembling the Quilt Top

1. Sew the blocks into 12 rows of five appliquéd blocks and five pieced blocks each, alternating the blocks in each row and from row to row. Note that the appliquéd blocks are facing the opposite direction in every other row.

2. For the inner border, sew three gold print 1½" x 42" strips together end to end. Repeat to make a total of three pieced strips. Trim two of the strips to 96½" long. Sew these strips to the sides of the quilt top. Trim the remaining pieced strip to 82½" long and stitch it to the bottom of the quilt top.

3. For the outer border, sew three red striped 5½" x 42" strips together end to end. Repeat to make a total of three pieced strips. Trim two of the strips to 97½" long. Sew these strips to the sides of the quilt top. Trim the remaining pieced strip to 92½" long and stitch it to the bottom of the quilt top.

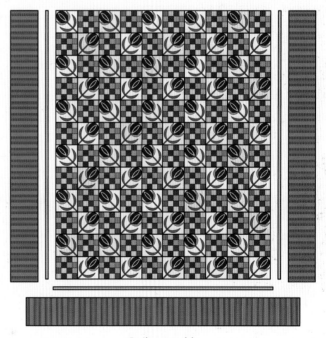

Quilt assembly

Finishing

Refer to "Quilting and Binding" on page 7 to layer the quilt top, batting, and backing. Quilt as desired. Bind the quilt using the red checked 1½" strips.

Love Knot Pillows

These long, knotted pillows are a fast and easy alternative to a pillow sham. Just a few simple seams and they're ready to go on the bed. You'll fall in love with this great look!

~Avis

Materials (for 2 pillows)

Yardage is based on 42"-wide fabric.

4¾ yards of red striped fabric (to coordinate with the "Pomegranate Christmas" quilt)

2 standard-size bed pillows

Cutting

From the *lengthwise* grain of the red striped fabric, cut:

2 rectangles, 77" x width of fabric

Instructions

For each pillow, fold the fabric rectangle in half lengthwise, right sides together, to make a rectangle approximately 21" wide and 77" long. Stitch across one short end and the long edge. Fold up the open end ½"; press. Then fold up the end 3" and press again. Stitch close to the folded edge. Turn the case right side out. Insert the pillow into the cover and push it all the way to the stitched end. Tie a simple knot at the open end, cinching up the knot close to the pillow.

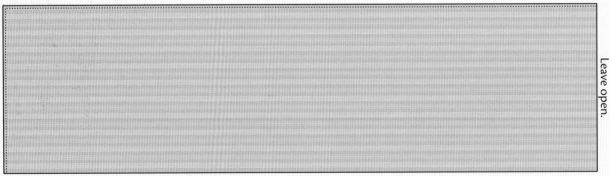

Leave open.

Fold

Finished pillow size: approximately 20½" x 73"

Pomegranate Pillow

This sweet little pillow is the perfect addition to your bedroom, especially when the "Pomegranate Christmas" quilt is on the bed. It would look equally inviting on a sofa or nestled in a wingback chair. Pillows are terrific for making a home warm and cozy.

~Avis

Materials

Yardage is based on 42"-wide fabric.

1 yard of red striped fabric for sashing, outer border, and pillow back

⅓ yard of light fabric for block backgrounds

¼ yard of red checked fabric for inner border

¼ yard of green print for stem and lower leaf appliqués

¼ yard of taupe print for upper leaf appliqués

¼ yard of red print for outer bud appliqués

⅛ yard of gold print for middle bud appliqués and cornerstone squares

⅛ yard of red-and-gold print for inner bud appliqués

⅓ yard of fabric for pillow-front backing

16" x 26" piece of batting

½ yard of paper-backed fusible web

12" x 22" pillow form

Cutting

The appliqué patterns are found on page 17. For more information on cutting pieces for fusible appliqué, refer to "Fusible Appliqué" on page 6.

From the light fabric, cut:
• 2 squares, 8½" x 8½"

From the green print, cut:
• 2 lower leaf appliqué shapes
• 2 stem appliqué shapes

From the taupe print, cut:
• 2 upper leaf appliqué shapes

From the red print, cut:
• 2 outer bud appliqué shapes

From the gold print, cut:
• 2 middle bud appliqué shapes
• 8 squares, 1½" x 1½"

From the red-and-gold print, cut:
• 2 inner bud appliqué shapes

From the red striped fabric, cut:
• 1 rectangle, 12½" x 18½"
• 1 rectangle, 12½" x 22½"
• 1 rectangle, 2½" x 8½"
• 2 rectangles, 1½" x 20½"
• 2 rectangles, 1½" x 10½"

From the red checked fabric, cut:
• 2 rectangles, 1½" x 18½"
• 2 rectangles, 1½" x 8½"

From the front-backing fabric, cut:
• 1 rectangle, 16" x 26"

Finished pillow size: 12" x 22"

Finished block size: 8" x 8"

Constructing the Blocks

Refer to "Fusible Appliqué" on page 6 and the photo above to position one of each of the appliqué shapes on an 8½" light background square. The end of the stem should be placed in the corner of the background square. When you are happy with the placement, fuse the shapes in place. Machine blanket stitch around each appliqué shape with matching thread. Repeat to make a total of two blocks. If you are using a directional background fabric, make sure that the pomegranate appliqué faces the opposite direction in the second block.

Make 2.

Assembling the Pillow

1 Stitch together the two appliquéd blocks and the red striped 2½" x 8½" rectangle. Make sure that one of your blocks is facing left and one is facing right.

2 Stitch red checked 1½" x 18½" rectangles to the top and bottom of the unit. Sew a gold print 1½" square to each end of the two red checked 1½" x 8½" rectangles. Sew these units to the sides.

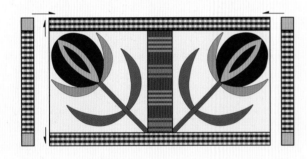

3 Sew red striped 1½" x 20½" rectangles to the top and bottom of this unit. Sew a gold print 1½" square to each end of the two red striped 1½" x 10½" rectangles. Sew these units to the sides.

4 Layer the front-backing rectangle with the batting and then the pillow top, right side up; baste the layers together. Quilt in the ditch around the appliqué shapes and the border strips. Stitch through all the layers, ⅛" from the pillow top outer edges. Trim the batting and backing even with the pillow top.

5 Press under ¼" on one short side of the red striped 12½" x 18½" rectangle. Turn under the pressed edge 1", press, and then stitch close to the first pressed edge. The piece should now measure 12½" x 17¼". Fold the red striped 12½" x 22½" piece in half, right sides together, so it measures 12½" x 11¼".

6 Lay the quilted pillow top right side up on a flat surface. Place the folded red striped rectangle over the quilt top, with the raw edges aligned on the right-hand side of the pillow top. Position the red striped 12½" x 17¼" rectangle over the folded piece, wrong side up, with the raw edge aligned with the left-hand side of the pillow top.

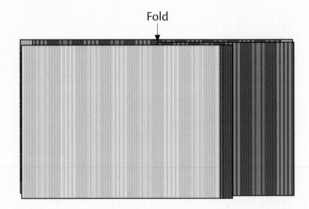

Fold

7 Stitch all the way around the pillow pieces; turn right side out. Insert the pillow form into the opening in the back.

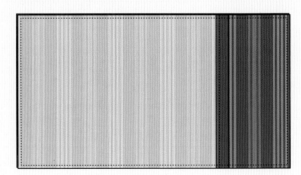

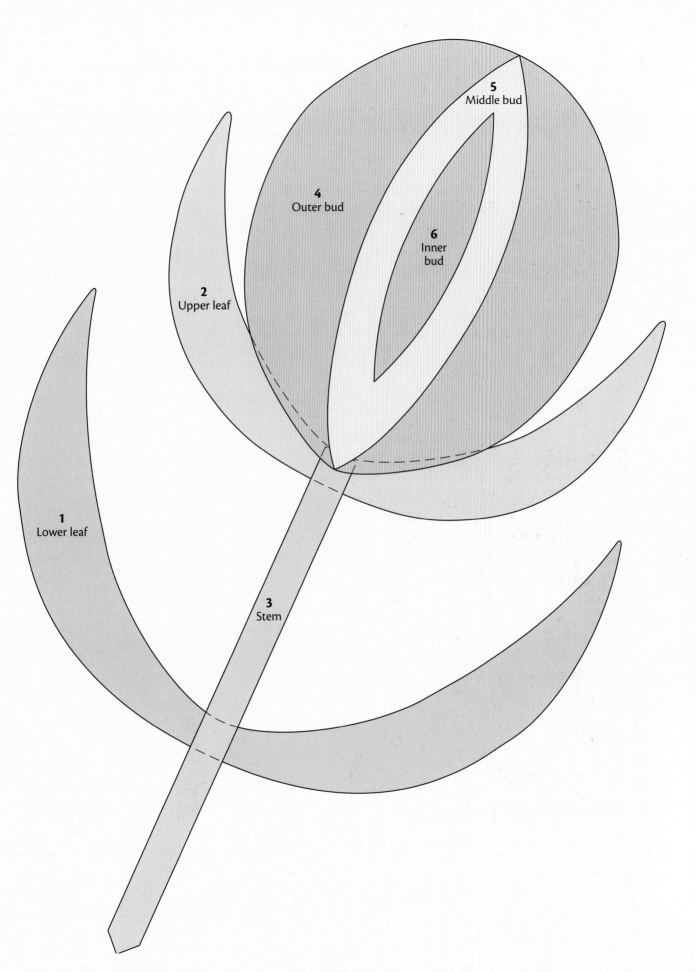

5
Middle bud

4
Outer bud

6
Inner
bud

2
Upper leaf

1
Lower leaf

3
Stem

A Warm Welcome

The pineapple is a traditional symbol of hospitality. This quilt
uses a simple pieced pineapple shape that is embellished with wool
and buttons. A pieced house block and a vintage-looking border
fabric were added to bid visitors a warm welcome.

~Tammy

Materials

Yardage is based on 42"-wide fabric.

1 yard of brown floral for outer border and binding

⅞ yard of cream print for block backgrounds

⅝ yard of taupe solid for sashing strips and flying-geese units

½ yard of taupe striped fabric for houses

⅜ yard of gold solid for pineapples

⅓ yard of pink print for inner border

¼ yard of dark brown checked fabric for house windows

⅛ yard of brown plaid for house roofs

⅛ yard of brown print for house chimneys

⅛ yard of red print for house doors

5" x 25" piece of green plaid felted wool for pineapple-top appliqués

6" x 10" piece of gold felted wool for pineapple accents

Scraps of 12 assorted green, pink, red, and brown fabrics for flying-geese units

2⅞ yards of fabric for backing

45" x 69" piece of batting

½ yard of paper-backed fusible web

24 tan and brown assorted buttons

Cutting

The appliqué pattern is found on page 25. For more information on cutting pieces for fusible appliqué, refer to "Fusible Appliqué" on page 6.

From the taupe striped fabric, cut:
• 6 strips, 1½" x 42"
• 15 rectangles, 1½" x 7½"
• 10 rectangles, 1½" x 3½"

From the dark brown checked fabric, cut:
• 4 strips, 1½" x 42"

From the red print, cut:
• 5 rectangles, 1½" x 4½"

From the cream print, cut:
• 4 rectangles, 4½" x 9½"
• 8 rectangles, 2½" x 13½"
• 28 squares, 2½" x 2½"
• 10 rectangles, 1½" x 17½"
• 5 rectangles, 1½" x 3½"
• 13 squares, 1½" x 1½"

From the brown plaid, cut:
• 5 rectangles, 2½" x 7½"

From the brown print, cut:
• 10 squares, 1½" x 1½"

From the gold solid, cut:
• 4 rectangles, 5½" x 13½"

Quilted by Sue Urich

Finished quilt size: 39" x 63"

Finished block size: 9" x 17"

From the green plaid wool, cut:
• 2 pineapple-top appliqué shapes and 2 reversed

From the taupe solid, cut:
• 2 rectangles, 2½" x 9½"
• 2 rectangles, 2½" x 8½"
• 3 rectangles, 2½" x 7½"
• 3 rectangles, 2½" x 6½"
• 3 rectangles, 2½" x 4½"
• 5 rectangles, 2½" x 3½"
• 2 squares, 2½" x 2½"
• 5 strips, 1½" x 42"; crosscut into 120 squares, 1½" x 1½"

From the assorted scraps, cut:
• 60 rectangles, 1½" x 2½"

From the pink print, cut:
• 2 strips, 1½" x 31½"
• 3 strips, 1½" x 42"

From the brown floral, cut:
• 2 strips, 3½" x 33½"
• 4 strips, 3½" x 42"
• 6 strips, 1½" x 42"

Constructing the House Blocks

① Alternately sew together four taupe striped 1½" x 42" strips and three brown checked 1½" x 42" strips to make strip set A. Alternate the end you begin sewing with each strip to keep your strip unit straight. Press the seam allowances in one direction. Crosscut the strip unit into 10 segments, 3½" wide.

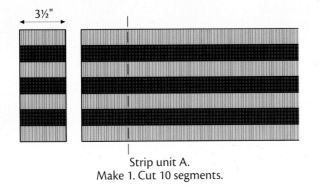

Strip unit A.
Make 1. Cut 10 segments.

② Sew the remaining taupe striped 1½" x 42" strips to both long edges of the brown checked 1½" x 42" strip to make strip set B, following the same procedure as before. Press the seam allowances in one direction. Crosscut this strip unit into 10 segments, 3½" wide.

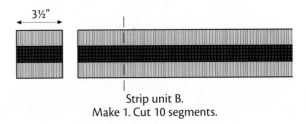

Strip unit B.
Make 1. Cut 10 segments.

③ Alternately stitch together two strip set A segments and three taupe striped 1½" x 7½" rectangles. Repeat to make a total of five window units.

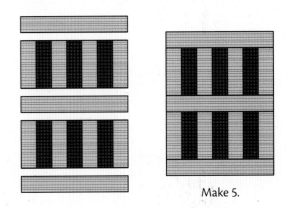

Make 5.

④ Stitch taupe striped 1½" x 3½" rectangles to each strip set B segment as shown. Join one of these units to each long side of a red 1½" x 4½" rectangle. Repeat to make a total of five door units.

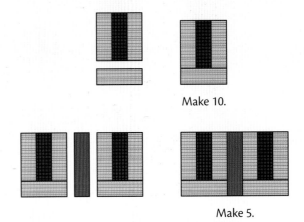

Make 10.

Make 5.

⑤ Sew a door unit to the bottom of each window unit.

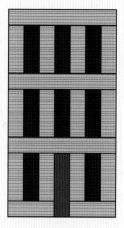

Make 5.

⑥ Refer to "Folded Corners" on page 5 to fold a cream print 2½" square in half diagonally and place it on one end of a brown plaid 2½" x 7½" rectangle, with the marked line in the direction shown. Stitch on the marked line, trim ¼" from the stitching, and press the resulting triangle over the seam. Repeat on the opposite end, changing the stitching angle as shown. Repeat to make a total of five roof units.

Make 5.

⑦ To make the chimney units, sew brown print 1½" squares to opposite sides of a cream print 1½" square. Add a cream print 1½" x 3½" rectangle to the top of this unit. Sew cream print 2½" squares to the short sides of the unit. Repeat to make a total of five units.

Make 5.

⑧ Add a chimney unit to the top of each roof unit. Join one of these units to the top of each window/door unit from step 5. Sew cream print 1½" x 17½" rectangles to the sides of the house units to complete the block. Repeat to make a total of five House blocks.

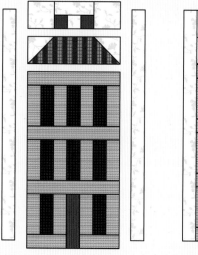 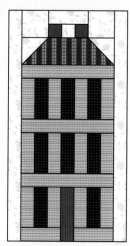

Make 5.

Constructing the Pineapple Blocks

① Refer to "Folded Corners" on page 5 to fold two cream print 1½" squares in half diagonally and place them on the lower left and right corners of a gold 5½" x 13½" rectangle. Stitch on the marked line, trim ¼" from the stitching, and press the resulting triangles over the seam.

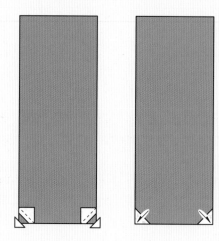

② Repeat step 1 with two cream print 2½" squares, placing them in the upper corners of the gold rectangle.

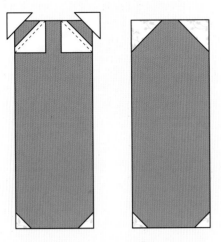

③ Sew cream print 2½" x 13½" rectangles to the sides of the unit. Add a cream print 4½" x 9½" rectangle to the top of the unit.

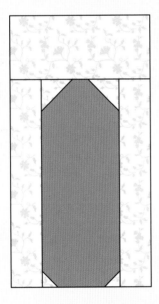

④ Appliqué a pineapple-top shape to the top of the pineapple, referring to the photo on page 20 for placement help.

⑤ Repeat steps 1–4 to make a total of four blocks.

⑥ From the remaining paper-backed fusible web, cut a 6" x 10" piece. Follow the manufacturer's instructions to fuse it to the gold wool piece. From the prepared wool, cut 32 rectangles, ¼" x 4", using your rotary cutter. Remove the paper backing and position eight of the strips down the center of one pineapple, crossing the strips as shown; fuse in place. Stitch the strips in place. We used a machine overlock stitch with variegated gold thread. Set the stitch width so that it is as wide as the wool strip. You could sew a blanket stitch on both edges of the strips if you prefer.

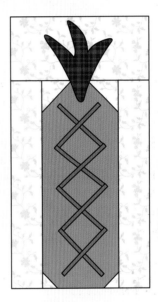

Making the Sashing Strips

① Refer to "Folded Corners" on page 5 to fold the 120 taupe solid 1½" squares in half diagonally. Lay one folded square on one end of an assorted scrap 1½" x 2½" rectangle. Stitch on the marked line, trim ¼" from the stitching, and press the resulting triangles over the seam. Repeat on the opposite end of the rectangle. Repeat to make a total of 60 flying-geese units.

Make 60.

2 Sew the flying-geese units and taupe solid rectangles and squares together as shown to make sashing units 1, 2, and 3.

4 For the outer border, sew the brown floral 3½" x 33½" strips to the top and bottom of the quilt top. Join the four brown floral 3½" x 42" strips end to end. From the pieced strip, cut two 3½" x 63½" strips and sew them to the sides of the quilt top.

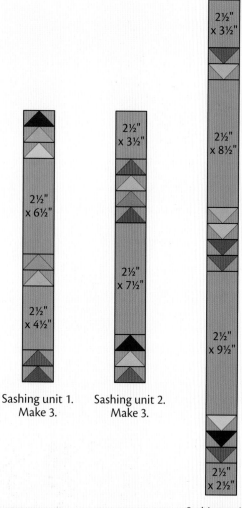

Sashing unit 1. Make 3.

Sashing unit 2. Make 3.

Sashing unit 3. Make 2.

Quilt assembly

Assembling the Quilt Top

1 Refer to the quilt assembly diagram to arrange the blocks and sashing unit 1 and 2 strips into three rows, alternating the blocks in each row and from row to row. Sew the blocks and strips in each row together.

2 Sew the rows together, adding a sashing unit 3 strip between each row.

3 For the inner border, sew the two pink print 1½" x 31½" strips to the top and bottom of the quilt top. Join the three pink print 1½" x 42" strips end to end. From the pieced strip, cut two 1½" x 57½" strips. Sew these strips to the sides of the quilt top.

Finishing

Refer to "Quilting and Binding" on page 7 to layer the quilt top, batting, and backing. Quilt as desired. Bind the quilt using the brown floral 1½" strips. Randomly stitch the buttons to each pineapple.

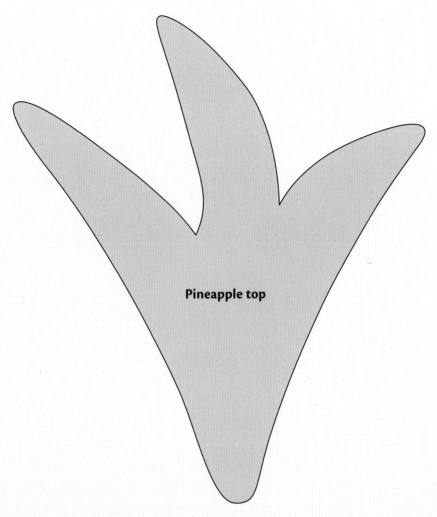

Pineapple top

He Loves Me, He Loves Me Not

Gerbera daisies are bright and colorful. Just imagine how much fun it would be to pull the petals out, one by one, deciding the fate of true love.

~Avis

Materials

Yardage is based on 42"-wide fabric.

⅓ yard *each* of pink, orange, yellow, red, and rose fabrics for flower appliqués

⅞ yard of light print for appliqué block backgrounds

⅞ yard of red polka-dot fabric for outer border, sashing squares, and binding

¼ yard *each* of pink print, green plaid, and taupe solid for pieced sashing strips and pieced inner border

⅓ yard of green print for bias stems and leaf appliqués

1⅔ yards of fabric for backing

42" x 54" piece of batting

1 yard of paper-backed fusible web

9 assorted buttons, 1⅜"-diameter

Cutting

The appliqué patterns are found on page 31. For more information on cutting pieces for fusible appliqué, refer to "Fusible Appliqué" on page 6. For information on cutting bias strips, refer to "Making and Applying Bias Stems" on page 6.

From the green print, cut:
• 9 bias strips, 1" x 10"
• 12 leaf appliqué shapes

From the light print, cut:
• 3 strips, 8½" x 42", crosscut into 9 rectangles, 8½" x 12½"

From *each* of the pink, orange, yellow, and red fabrics, cut:
• 2 flower appliqué shapes (8 total)

From the rose fabric, cut:
• 1 flower appliqué shape

From the pink print, cut:
• 3 strips, 2½" x 42"; crosscut into:
  - 24 squares, 2½" x 2½"
  - 24 rectangles, 1½" x 2½"

From the taupe solid, cut:
• 3 strips, 2½" x 42"; crosscut into:
  - 18 squares, 2½" x 2½"
  - 24 rectangles, 1½" x 2½"

From the green plaid, cut:
• 3 strips, 2½" x 42"; crosscut into:
  - 18 squares, 2½" x 2½"
  - 22 rectangles, 1½" x 2½"

From the red polka-dot fabric, cut:
• 2 strips, 3½" x 30½"
• 3 strips, 3½" x 42"
• 4 squares, 2½" x 2½"
• 5 strips, 1½" x 42"

Quilted by Sue Urich
Finished quilt size: 36" x 48"
Finished block size: 8" x 12"

Constructing the Blocks

1. Refer to "Making and Applying Bias Stems" on page 6 to use the green 1" x 10" bias strips to make the stem pieces. Trim three of these pieces to 8" long.

2. Position an 8" stem down the vertical center of three light print rectangles, one end of the stem even with the bottom edge of the rectangle. The upper end will be covered by the flower appliqué. Appliqué the stems in place by hand or machine. We used a machine blind hem stitch. Appliqué the remaining stems to the remaining six light print rectangles in the same manner, positioning three stems 1½" from the left side of the rectangles and three stems 1½" from the right side of the rectangles. Make a gentle curve in each of these stems that begins approximately 4½" from the bottom of the rectangle.

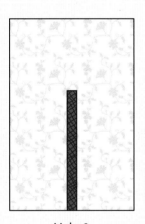

Make 3.

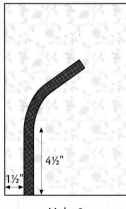

Make 3.

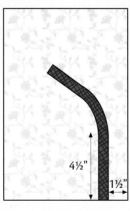

Make 3.

3. Refer to "Fusible Appliqué" on page 6 and the photo on page 28 to place a flower appliqué shape over the upper end of each stem. Rotate the flower shape on each block to create more interest. When you are happy with the placement, fuse the shapes in place. Next, position the leaf appliqués on the stems. Place one leaf on each of the six blocks with curved stems and two leaves on each of the three blocks with straight stems. When you are happy with the placement, fuse the shapes in place. Machine blanket stitch around the flowers and leaves with matching thread.

Constructing the Sashing Strips

1. Alternately sew together two pink 2½" squares, two taupe 2½" squares, and two green plaid 2½" squares as shown. Repeat to make a total of six vertical sashing strips.

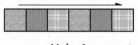

Make 6.

2. Sew together six pink 2½" squares, three green plaid 2½" squares, three taupe 2½" squares, and two red polka-dot 2½" squares in the order shown. Repeat to make a total of two horizontal sashing strips.

Make 2.

Assembling the Quilt Top

1. Refer to the assembly diagram to arrange one of each block variation and two vertical sashing strips into a row. Sew the pieces together. Repeat to make a total of three rows. Join the rows, adding a horizontal sashing strip between each row.

② For the inner borders, alternately stitch together the pink, taupe, and green plaid 1½" x 2½" rectangles. Use 14 rectangles for each top and bottom border and 21 rectangles for each side border. Sew the top and bottom borders to the top and bottom of the quilt top. Sew the side borders to the sides of the quilt top.

③ For the outer borders, sew the red polka-dot 3½" x 30½" strips to the top and bottom of the quilt top. Sew the three red polka-dot 3½" x 42" strips together end to end. From the pieced strip, cut two strips, 3½" x 48½", and sew them to the sides of the quilt top.

Finishing

Refer to "Quilting and Binding" on page 7 to layer the quilt top, batting, and backing. Quilt as desired. Bind the quilt with the red polka-dot 1½" strips. Sew a button to the center of each flower shape.

Quilt assembly

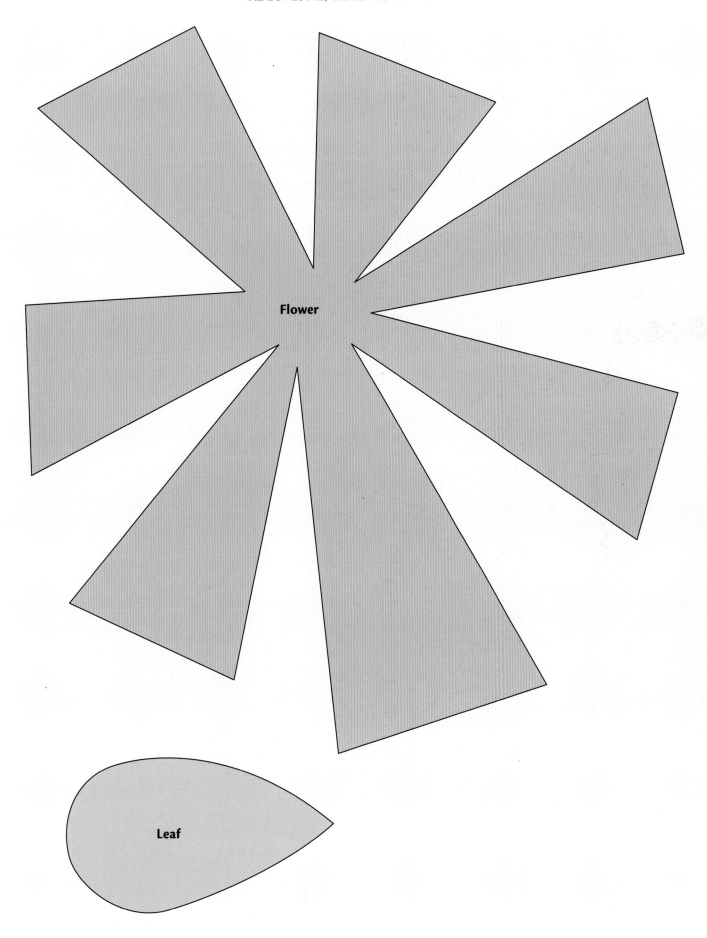

Flower

Leaf

My Best Sampler

This sampler contains a number of easy-to-sew units and a touch of appliqué. Flying-geese units make a nice frame for the quilt.

~Avis

Quilted by Sue Urich
Finished quilt size: 38" x 38"

Materials

Yardage is based on 42"-wide fabric.

⅛ yard *each* of 10 assorted dark fabrics for flying-geese and four-patch units

⅛ yard *each* of 10 assorted light fabrics for flying-geese units

⅛ yard *each* of 5 assorted dark fabrics for Churn Dash blocks

⅛ yard *each* of 5 assorted light fabrics for Churn Dash blocks

⅛ yard *each* of 4 assorted red fabrics for flag

⅛ yard *each* of 3 assorted light fabrics for flag

⅓ yard of brown plaid for house

⅓ yard of light fabric for letter and number sections backgrounds

⅓ yard of charcoal print for letter and number appliqués

⅓ yard of charcoal plaid for inner border and Churn Dash section spacer pieces

¼ yard of blue fabric for flag

¼ yard of gold fabric for star appliqués

¼ yard of taupe striped fabric for flower section background

¼ yard of green print for hill appliqué

¼ yard of green plaid for stem appliqués

¼ yard of pink print for flower appliqués

¼ yard of light fabric for house section background

¼ yard of black print for roof

⅛ yard of light yellow print for windows

⅛ yard of blue fabric for door

⅛ yard of rust print for chimneys

⅛ yard of green print for leaf appliqués

⅛ yard of pink solid for flower center appliqués

1⅜ yards of fabric for backing

¼ yard of fabric for binding

44" x 44" square of batting

1 yard of paper-backed fusible web

Cutting

The appliqué patterns are found on pages 39–41. For more information on cutting pieces for fusible appliqué, refer to "Fusible Appliqué" on page 6.

From the 4 assorted red fabrics, cut a *total* of:
• 2 strips, 1½" x 20½"
• 2 strips, 1½" x 32½"

From the 3 assorted light fabrics for flag, cut a *total* of:
• 2 strips, 1½" x 20½"
• 1 strip, 1½" x 32½"

From the blue fabric for flag, cut:
• 1 rectangle, 4½" x 12½"

From the gold fabric, cut:
• 4 star appliqué shapes

From the green plaid, cut:
- 1 bias strip, ¾" x 10½"
- 1 bias strip, ¾" x 4"
- 1 bias strip, ¾" x 6½"

From the taupe striped fabric, cut:
- 1 rectangle, 6½" x 20½"

From the green print for hill, cut:
- 1 hill appliqué shape

From the green print for leaves, cut:
- 4 leaf appliqué shapes

From the pink print, cut:
- 1 *each* of the small, medium, and large flower appliqué shapes

From the pink solid, cut:
- 1 large flower center appliqué shape
- 2 small/medium flower center appliqué shapes

From the light fabric for letter and number section, cut:
- 2 rectangles, 8½" x 11½"
- 1 rectangle, 2½" x 4½"
- 1 rectangle, 1½" x 4½"

From the charcoal print, cut:
- 1 *each* of A, B, C, 1, 2, and 3 appliqué shapes

From the 10 assorted dark fabrics for flying-geese and four-patch units, cut a *total* of:
- 8 squares, 2½" x 2½"
- 144 rectangles, 1½" x 2½"

From the light fabric for house background, cut:
- 1 rectangle, 3½" x 7½"
- 4 squares, 3½" x 3½"
- 2 rectangles, 1½" x 15½"

From the black print, cut:
- 1 rectangle, 3½" x 15½"

From the rust print, cut:
- 2 rectangles, 1½" x 3½"

From the brown plaid, cut:
- 1 rectangle, 2½" x 15½"
- 2 rectangles, 2½" x 6½"
- 2 rectangles, 2½" x 4½"
- 2 rectangles, 2½" x 3½"
- 1 rectangle, 1½" x 15½"
- 4 rectangles, 1½" x 4½"
- 5 rectangles, 1½" x 3½"

From the light yellow print, cut:
- 6 rectangles, 1½" x 3½"
- 4 rectangles, 1½" x 4½"

From the blue fabric for door, cut:
- 1 rectangle, 3½" x 6½"

From *each* of 4 of the assorted dark fabrics for Churn Dash blocks, cut:
- 2 squares, 2⅞" x 2⅞"; cut each square once diagonally to yield four triangles (16 total)
- 4 squares, 1½" x 1½" (16 total)

From the remaining assorted dark fabric for Churn Dash blocks, cut:
- 2 squares, 2⅞" x 2⅞"; cut each square once diagonally to yield four triangles
- 2 rectangles, 1½" x 4½"
- 2 squares, 1½" x 1½"

From *each* of 4 of the assorted light fabrics for Churn Dash blocks, cut:
- 2 squares, 2⅞" x 2⅞"; cut each square once diagonally to yield four triangles (16 total)
- 5 squares, 1½" x 1½" (20 total)

From the remaining assorted light fabric for Churn Dash blocks, cut:
- 2 squares, 2⅞" x 2⅞"; cut each square once diagonally to yield four triangles
- 3 rectangles, 1½" x 4½"
- 2 squares, 1½" x 1½"

From the charcoal plaid, cut:
- 2 strips, 1½" x 32½"
- 2 strips, 1½" x 34½"
- 4 rectangles, 1½" x 5½"

From the 10 assorted light fabrics for flying-geese units, cut a _total_ of:
- 144 matching pairs of squares, 1½" x 1½" (288 total)

From the fabric for binding, cut:
- 4 strips, 1½" x 42"

Constructing the Flag Section

① Sew the two red 1½" x 20½" strips and the two light 1½" x 20½" strips together along the long edges, alternating colors. Add the blue 4½" x 12½" rectangle to the left side of the joined strips.

② Sew the two red 1½" x 32½" strips and the light 1½" x 32½" strip together along the long edges. Add this unit to the bottom of the unit from step 1.

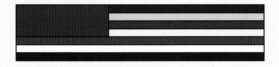

③ Refer to "Fusible Appliqué" on page 6 and the photo on page 33 to position the star appliqué shapes on the blue rectangle of the unit. When you are happy with the placement, fuse the shapes in place. Machine blanket-stitch around each star with matching thread.

Constructing the Flower Section

① Refer to "Making and Applying Bias Stems" on page 6 to use the green plaid strips to make the stem pieces. Refer to the photo on page 33 as needed to position the 10½"-long stem down the middle of the taupe striped 6½" x 20½" rectangle, placing the end approximately 4¾" from

the bottom edge. Position the 4"-long stem on the left side of the center stem and the 6½"-long stem on the right side of the center stem. The ends of these stems should be ½" lower than the center stem. Check the placement by temporarily positioning the hill and flower appliqué shapes in place. When you are happy with the stem placement, remove the hill and flower appliqués and machine appliqué the stems in place with a blind hem stitch.

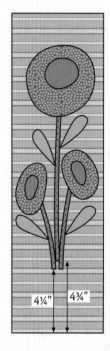

② Refer to "Fusible Applique" and the photo to place the hill appliqué over the bottom end of the stems, aligning the straight edge of the appliqué with the bottom edge of the rectangle. Position the leaves along the stems next. Then, position the flower appliqués over the upper end of the stems, placing the large flower shape over the center stem, the medium flower shape on the right stem, and the small flower shape on the left stem. Finally, position the flower center shapes over the appropriate flower. When you are happy with the placement, fuse the shapes in place. Machine blanket stitch around each appliqué with matching thread.

Constructing the Letters and Numbers Section

1. Refer to "Fusible Appliqué" and the photo to position the A, B, and C appliqué shapes on a light 8½" x 11½" rectangle. Position the 1, 2, and 3 appliqué shapes on the remaining light 8½" x 11½" rectangle. When you are happy with the placement, fuse the shapes in place. Machine blanket stitch around each appliqué with matching thread.

2. Arrange four assorted dark 2½" squares into two rows of two squares each. Stitch the squares in each row together, and then stitch the rows together. Repeat to make a total of two four-patch units.

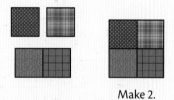

Make 2.

3. Sew the four-patch units, the light 1½" x 4½" rectangle, and the light 2½" x 4½" rectangle together.

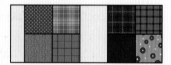

4. Sew the unit from step 3 and the appliquéd units together.

Constructing the House Section

1. Sew a rust print 1½" x 3½" rectangle to each end of the light 3½" x 7½" rectangle. Add a light 3½" square to each end of this unit, and then join a light 1½" x 15½" rectangle to the top to complete the chimney unit.

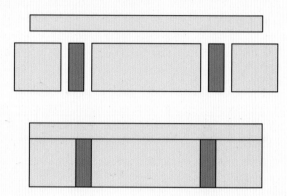

2. Refer to "Folded Corners" on page 5 to fold the remaining two light 3½" squares in half diagonally; place one on each end of the black 3½" x 15½" rectangle, with the marked lines in the directions shown. Stitch on the marked lines, trim ¼" from the stitching, and press the resulting triangles over the seams to complete the roof unit.

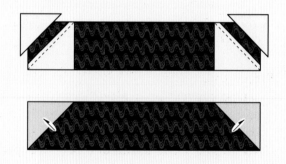

3. Sew the roof unit to the bottom of the chimney unit.

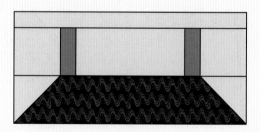

④ Alternately stitch together four light yellow 1½" x 3½" rectangles and three brown plaid 1½" x 3½" rectangles. Add brown plaid 2½" x 3½" rectangles to both ends of this unit. Join a light yellow 1½" x 3½" rectangle and then a brown plaid 1½" x 3½" rectangle to each end. Sew the brown plaid 1½" x 15½" rectangle to the top of this unit and the brown plaid 2½" x 15½" rectangle to the bottom. Sew this unit to the bottom of the chimney/roof unit.

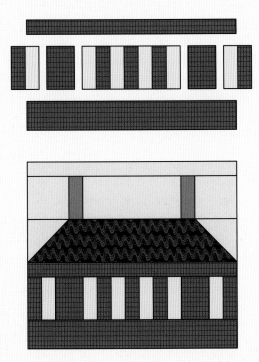

⑤ Sew light yellow 1½" x 4½" rectangles to the long edges of a brown plaid 2½" x 4½" rectangle. Add a brown plaid 1½" x 4½" rectangle to each end of the unit. Stitch a brown plaid 2½" x 6½" rectangle to the bottom of this unit. Repeat to make a total of two units.

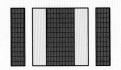 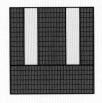

Make 2.

⑥ Sew the units from step 5 to the long edges of the blue 3½" x 6½" rectangle. Sew this unit to the bottom of the units from step 4. Add the remaining light 1½" x 15½" rectangle to the bottom.

Constructing the Churn Dash Section

① Using the 2⅞" triangles cut from the four assorted dark and four assorted light fabrics, stitch together a light and a dark triangle. Repeat to make four matching half-square-triangle units.

Make 4.

② Using the same light and dark fabrics, sew a light 1½" square to a dark 1½" square. Repeat to make four matching two-patch units.

Make 4.

③ Sew the half-square-triangle units, the two-patch units, and the remaining matching light 1½" square together.

④ Repeat steps 1–3 to make a total of four square Churn Dash blocks.

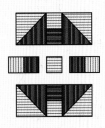 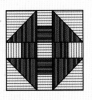

⑤ Using the triangles, squares, and rectangles cut from the remaining light and dark fabrics, repeat step 1 to make four matching half-square-triangle units. Repeat step 2 to make two two-patch units with the light and dark 1½" squares. Sew each dark 1½" x 4½" rectangle to a light 1½" x 4½" rectangle. Sew all of these units and the remaining light 1½" x 4½" rectangle together to make a rectangular Churn Dash block.

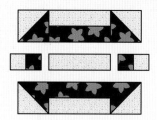

⑥ Sew the Churn Dash blocks and the four charcoal plaid 1½" x 5½" rectangles together.

Assembling the Quilt Top

① Refer to the quilt assembly diagram to sew the flower section to the left side of the house section. Add the letters and numbers section to the right side of the house section. Join the flag section to the top and the churn dash section to the bottom.

② Sew the charcoal plaid 1½" x 32½" strips to the top and bottom of the quilt top. Sew the charcoal plaid 1½" x 34½" strips to the sides of the quilt top.

③ Construct the flying-geese units for the outer border. Refer to "Folded Corners" to fold two matching light 1½" squares in half diagonally. Place one square on one end of a dark 1½" x 2½" rectangle. Stitch on the marked line, trim ¼" from the stitching, and press the resulting triangle over the seam. Repeat with the remain-

ing square on the opposite end of the rectangle, changing the stitching angle as shown. Repeat to make a total of 144 flying-geese units.

Make 144.

④ Refer to the quilt assembly diagram to stitch 34 flying-geese units together along the long edges, with all of the units pointing in the same direction. Stitch the border to the bottom of the quilt top, with the arrows pointing to the left. Repeat to make two strips using 36 flying-geese units. Sew one strip to the right edge of the quilt top, with the arrows pointing up. Add the remaining strip to the top of the quilt top, with the arrows pointing to the left. Join the remaining 38 flying-geese units and sew the strip to the left edge of the quilt top, with the arrows pointing down.

Quilt assembly

Finishing

Refer to "Quilting and Binding" on page 7 to layer the quilt top, batting, and backing. Quilt as desired. Bind the quilt with the 1½" binding strips.

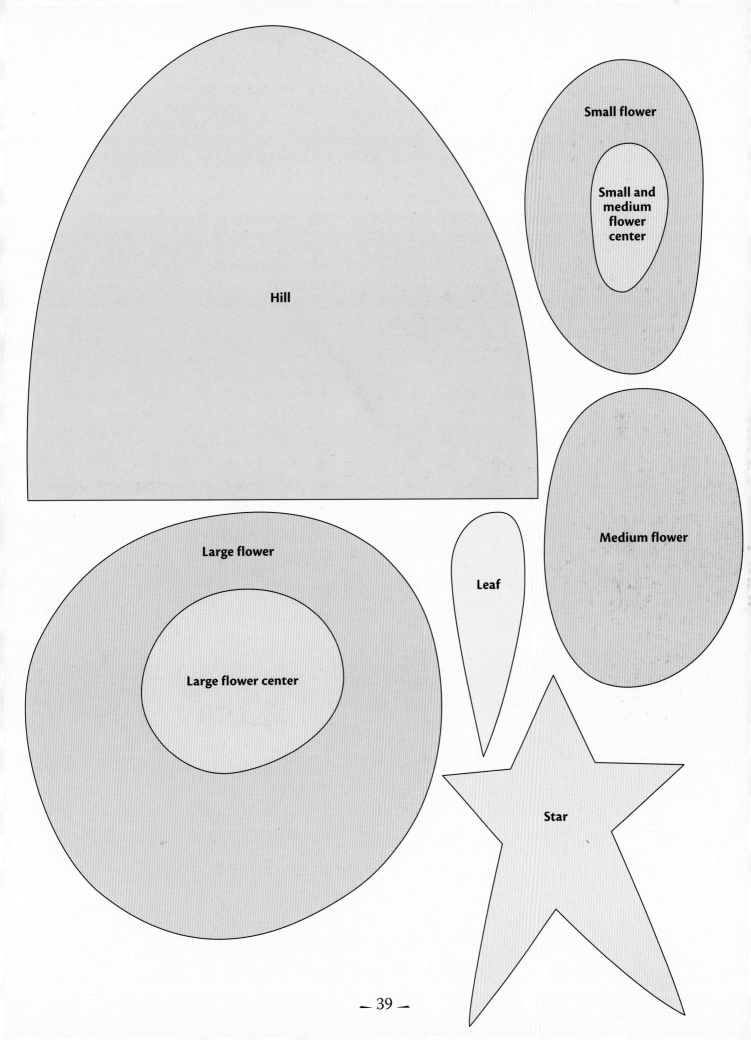

Hill

Small flower

Small and medium flower center

Medium flower

Large flower

Large flower center

Leaf

Star

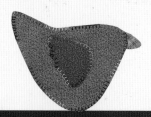

Bloom Door Banner

I love to make quilts that depict the seasons. This machine-pieced and appliquéd banner is easy to complete and will add a breath of spring to your home. The touch of rickrack is a gentle reminder of my Grandma, who had a candy tin that was filled with assorted scraps of rickrack in a rainbow of colors. I still have that candy tin and the rickrack, which is much too precious to me to use.

~Tammy

Quilted by Sue Urich

Finished banner size: 18" x 42"

Materials

Yardage is based on 42"-wide fabric.

½ yard of light blue print for background

½ yard of dark blue print for outer border and binding

⅓ yard of pink checked fabric for inner border and letter appliqués

¼ yard of tan solid for house

¼ yard of green print for ground

¼ yard *total* of 2 different green prints for leaf appliqués

¼ yard of medium blue print for bird appliqué

¼ yard of yellow print for outer sun appliqué

¼ yard *total* of 6 assorted pink prints for flower appliqués

⅛ yard of brown print for door and window trim

⅛ yard of green striped fabric for flower stems

Scrap of pale yellow fabric, at least 3¾" x 5", for window

Scrap of dark brown fabric, at least 1" x 10", for roof appliqué

Scrap of dark blue fabric, at least 2½" square, for bird's wing appliqué

Scrap of yellow fabric, at least 4" square, for sun center appliqué

Scrap of orange fabric, at least 1" square, for bird's beak appliqué

1½ yards of fabric for backing

24" x 48" piece of batting

1 yard of paper-backed fusible web

2 yards of ecru ⅜"-wide rickrack

Cutting

The appliqué patterns are found on pages 48 and 49. For more information on cutting pieces for fusible appliqué, refer to "Fusible Appliqué" on page 6.

From the light blue print, cut:
• 1 rectangle, 8½" x 9½"
• 1 square, 5½" x 5½"
• 1 rectangle, 4½" x 14½"
• 1 rectangle, 4½" x 6½"
• 1 rectangle, 3½" x 18½"
• 1 rectangle, 2½" x 22½"
• 1 rectangle, 2½" x 18½"

From the tan solid, cut:
• 1 rectangle, 5½" x 6½"
• 1 rectangle, 3½" x 13½"
• 1 rectangle, 3½" x 5½"
• 2 rectangles, 1½" x 8½"

From the pale yellow, cut:
• 4 rectangles, 1¼" x 3¾"

From the brown print, cut:
- 1 rectangle, 2½" x 13½"
- 2 rectangles, 1" x 8½"
- 1 rectangle, 1" x 7½"
- 2 rectangles, 1" x 2½"
- 2 rectangles, 1" x 1¼"

From the green striped fabric, cut:
- 1 rectangle, 1½" x 22½"
- 1 rectangle, 1½" x 18½"

From the green print for ground, cut:
- 1 rectangle, 4½" x 14½"

From the dark brown, cut:
- 1 roof appliqué shape

From the 2 green prints for leaves, cut a *total* of:
- 7 leaf appliqué shapes

From the 6 assorted pink prints, cut a *total* of:
- 7 flower appliqué shapes
- 7 flower center appliqué shapes

From the medium blue print, cut:
- 1 bird appliqué shape

From the dark blue, cut:
- 1 wing appliqué shape

From the orange fabric, cut:
- 1 beak appliqué shape

From the yellow print for outer sun, cut:
- 1 outer sun appliqué shape

From the yellow fabric for sun center, cut:
- 1 sun center appliqué shape

From the pink checked fabric, cut:
- 2 strips, 1" x 15½"
- 2 strips, 1" x 38½"
- 1 *each* of appliqué shapes B, L, and M
- 2 of appliqué shape O
- 1 exclamation point appliqué shape

From the dark blue print, cut:
- 2 strips, 2" x 18½"
- 2 strips, 2" x 39½"
- 4 strips, 1½" x 42"

Constructing the House Section

① Refer to "Folded Corners" on page 5 to fold the light blue 5½" square in half diagonally and place it on the tan 5½" x 6½" rectangle, with the marked line in the direction shown and aligning the top and side edges. Stitch on the marked line, trim ¼" from the stitching, and press the resulting triangle over the seam to complete the roof unit.

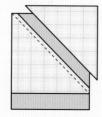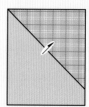

② Sew pale yellow 1¼" x 3¾" rectangles to the long edges of a brown 1" x 1¼" rectangle. Repeat to make a total of two windowpane units.

Make 2.

③ Stitch a windowpane unit to each side of the brown 1" x 7½" rectangle. Add brown 1" x 2½" rectangles to the top and bottom of this unit.

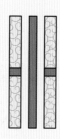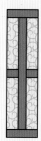

④ Sew a brown 1" x 8½" rectangle to each side of the step 3 unit, and then add a tan 1½" x 8½" rectangle to each side. Join the tan 3½" x 5½" rectangle to the bottom to complete the window unit.

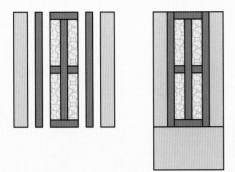

Constructing the Flower Section

① Sew the light blue 2½" x 18½" rectangle to the left edge of the green striped 1½" x 18½" rectangle and the light blue 3½" x 18½" rectangle to the right edge. Add the light blue 4½" x 6½" rectangle to the top of this unit.

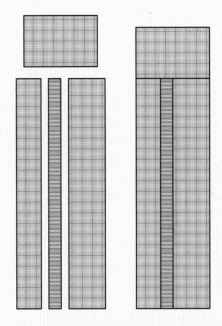

⑤ Sew the brown 2½" x 13½" rectangle and the tan 3½" x 13½" rectangle together. Add this unit to the bottom of the window unit. Sew the roof unit to the top of the window unit.

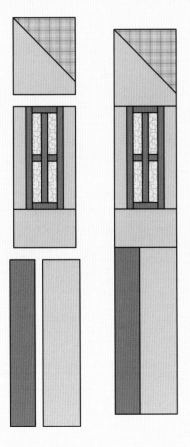

② To the left edge of the unit from step 1, add the green striped 1½" x 22½" rectangle and then the light blue 2½" x 22½" rectangle.

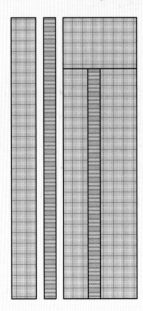

3 Add the light blue 8½" x 9½" rectangle to the top of the unit from step 2.

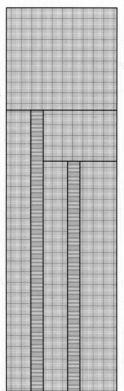

Joining the Sections

Sew the flower section to the right edge of the house section. Add the light blue 4½" x 14½" rectangle to the top of the joined sections and the green print 4½" x 14½" rectangle to the bottom.

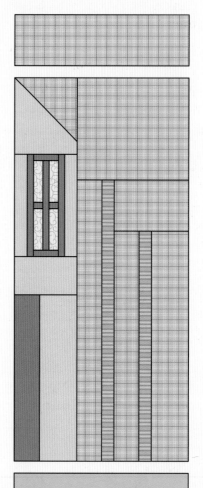

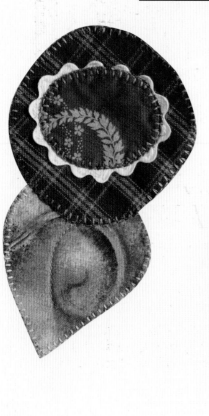

Appliquéing

Refer to "Fusible Appliqué" on page 6 and the photo on page 43 to position each appliqué shape on the quilt top as indicated at right. When you are happy with the placement, fuse the shapes in place. Machine blanket stitch around each appliqué with matching thread.

1. Appliqué the roof shape to the diagonal seam at the top of the house section.

2. Appliqué the leaves and outer flower shapes to the green striped stems.

3. Cut seven pieces of rickrack approximately 8½" long. Lay a flower center appliqué on top of each outer flower. Tuck the rickrack under the edge of the flower center, overlapping the ends and trimming if necessary. Fuse the flower center in place and then appliqué around the flower center edges.

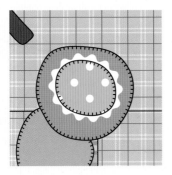

4. Position the bird at the top of the short flower stem. Tuck the beak under the body piece, and then add the wing to the top of the body. Fuse, and then appliqué the pieces in place.

5. Position the letters, exclamation point, and outer sun in the area above the house and flower sections. Appliqué the outer sun in place, and then appliqué the sun center to the outer sun. Appliqué the letters and exclamation point in place.

Adding the Borders

1. Stitch the pink checked 1" x 38½" strips to the sides of the quilt top. Sew pink checked 1" x 15½" strips to the top and bottom of the quilt top.

2. Sew the dark blue 2" x 39½" strips to the sides of the quilt top. Sew the dark blue 2" x 18½" strips to the top and bottom of the quilt top.

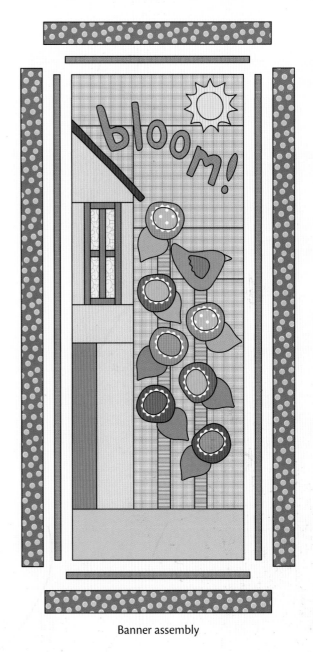

Banner assembly

Finishing

Refer to "Quilting and Binding" on page 7 to layer the quilt top, batting, and backing. Quilt as desired. Bind the quilt with the dark blue 1½" strips.

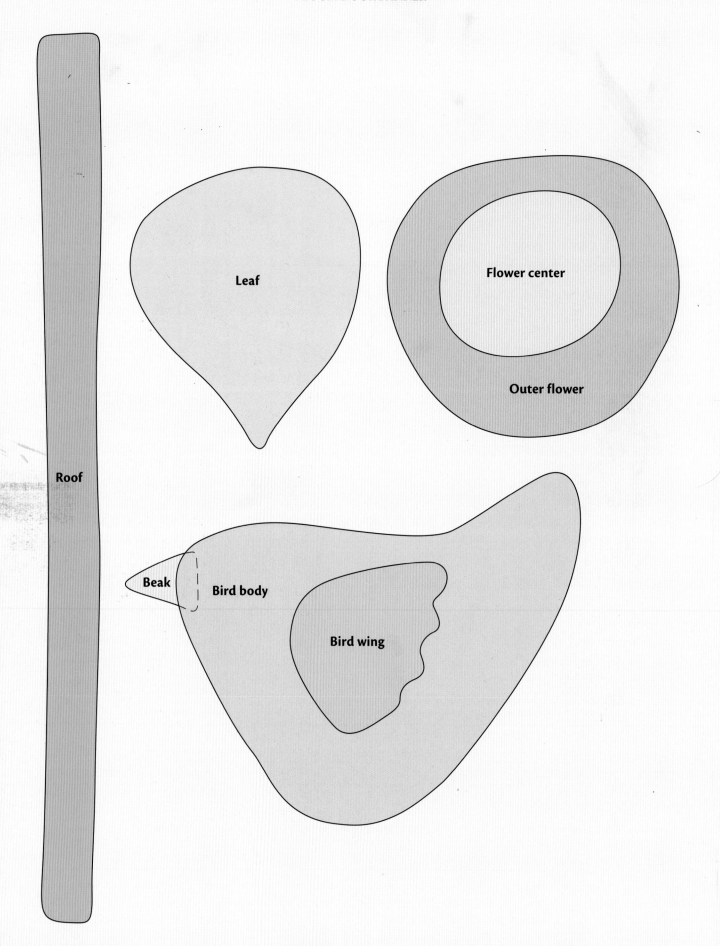

Roof

Leaf

Flower center

Outer flower

Beak

Bird body

Bird wing

Outer sun

Sun center

Liberty Door Banner

The dark sky in this door banner comes to life with a burst of fireworks.
Strips of wool are stitched down with metallic thread to give this quilt a
little extra sparkle. Stitch this one up to adorn your house for summer.

~Tammy

Quilted by Sue Urich

Finished banner size: 18" x 42"

Materials

Yardage is based on 42"-wide fabric.

½ yard of navy print 1 for background

¼ yard of navy plaid for outer border

¼ yard of red-and-cream print for inner border
and outer-border corner squares

¼ yard of light blue print for house

¼ yard of green print for ground

¼ yard of red striped fabric for window trim and
letter appliqués

⅛ yard of light gray solid for flagpole

⅛ yard of red fabric for flag stripes

⅛ yard of cream fabric for flag stripes

⅛ yard of red checked fabric for door and roof
appliqués

4" x 5" piece of off-white felted wool for fireworks

Scrap of dark gray fabric, at least 3¾" x 5", for
windows

Scrap of blue print fabric, at least 3½" square,
for flag

¼ yard of navy print 2 for binding

1½ yards of fabric for backing

24" x 48" piece of batting

½ yard of paper-backed fusible web

Silver metallic thread

Cutting

*The appliqué patterns are found on page 55. For
more information on cutting pieces for fusible appliqué, refer to "Fusible Appliqué" on page 6.*

From navy print 1, cut:
- 1 rectangle, 7½" x 19½"
- 1 rectangle, 6½" x 9½"
- 1 square, 5½" x 5½"
- 1 rectangle, 4½" x 14½"
- 1 rectangle, 2" x 24½"

From the light blue print, cut:
- 1 rectangle, 5½" x 6½"
- 1 rectangle, 3½" x 13½"
- 1 rectangle, 3½" x 5½"
- 2 rectangles, 1½" x 8½"

From the dark gray fabric, cut:
- 4 rectangles, 1¼" x 3¾"

From the red striped fabric, cut:
- 2 rectangles, 1" x 8½"
- 1 rectangle, 1" x 7½"
- 2 rectangles, 1" x 2½"
- 2 rectangles, 1" x 1¼"
- 1 *each* of appliqué shapes L, I, B, E, R, T, and Y

From the red checked fabric, cut:
- 1 rectangle, 2½" x 13½"
- 1 roof appliqué shape

From the red fabric, cut:
• 1 rectangle, 1½" x 7½"
• 2 rectangles, 1½" x 4½"

From the cream fabric, cut:
• 1 rectangle, 1½" x 7½"
• 1 rectangle, 1½" x 4½"

From the blue print scrap, cut:
• 1 square, 3½" x 3½"

From the light gray solid, cut:
• 1 rectangle, 1" x 24½"

From the green print, cut:
• 1 rectangle, 4½" x 14½"

From the red-and-cream print, cut:
• 2 strips, 1" x 14½"
• 2 strips, 1" x 39½"
• 4 squares, 2" x 2"

From the navy plaid, cut:
• 2 strips, 2" x 39½"
• 2 strips, 2" x 15½"

From navy print 2, cut:
• 4 strips, 1½" x 42"

Constructing the House Section

① Refer to "Folded Corners" on page 5 to fold the 5½" navy print 1 square in half diagonally and place it on the 5½" x 6½" light blue rectangle, with the marked line in the direction shown and aligning the top and side edges. Stitch on the marked line, trim ¼" from the stitching, and press the resulting triangle over the seam to complete the roof unit.

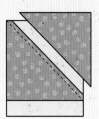

② Sew 1¼" x 3¾" dark gray rectangles to the long edges of a 1" x 1¼" red striped rectangle. Repeat to make a total of two windowpane units.

Make 2.

③ Stitch a windowpane unit to each side of the 1" x 7½" red striped rectangle. Add 1" x 2½" red striped rectangles to the top and bottom of this unit.

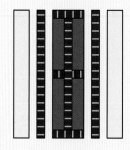

④ Sew a 1" x 8½" red striped rectangle to each side of the unit from step 3, and then add a 1½" x 8½" light blue rectangle to each side. Join the 3½" x 5½" light blue rectangle to the bottom to complete the window unit.

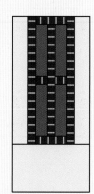

⑤ Sew the 2½" x 13½" red checked rectangle and the 3½" x 13½" light blue rectangle together. Add this unit to the bottom of the window unit. Sew the roof unit to the top of the window unit.

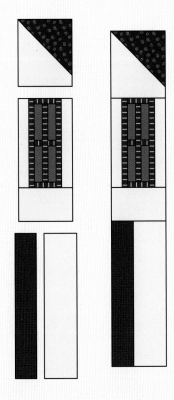

Constructing the Flag Section

① Alternately stitch together two 1½" x 4½" red rectangles and one 1½" x 4½" cream rectangle. Add the 3½" blue print square to the left side of this unit. Sew the 1½" x 7½" cream rectangle and the 1½" x 7½" red rectangle together. Add this unit to the bottom.

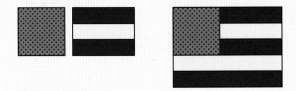

② Sew the 7½" x 19½" navy print 1 rectangle to the bottom of the unit from step 1. Stitch the 1" x 24½" light gray strip to the left side of the flag unit. Add the 2" x 24½" navy print 1 rectangle to the left side of this unit.

Join the 6½" x 9½" navy print 1 rectangle to the top.

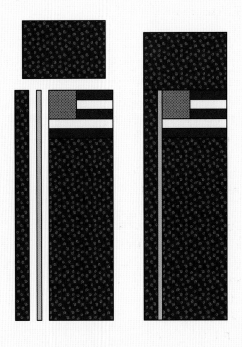

Joining the Sections

Sew the flag section to the right edge of the house section. Add the 4½" x 14½" navy print 1 rectangle to the top of the joined sections and the 4½" x 14½" green rectangle to the bottom.

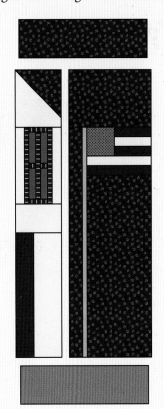

Appliquéing

Refer to "Fusible Appliqué" on page 6 and the photo on page 51 to position and fuse the appliqué shapes on the quilt top.

①　Position the roof appliqué across the diagonal seam at the top of the house section. Fuse the shape in place, and then machine appliqué around it with a blanket stitch and matching thread.

②　Position the letters on the area below the flag sections. Appliqué them in place with a blanket stitch and matching thread.

③　From the remaining paper-backed fusible web, cut a 4" x 5" piece. Follow the manufacturer's instructions to fuse it to the off-white felted wool piece. From the prepared wool, cut 12 rectangles, ¼" x 5", using your rotary cutter. Remove the paper backing and position the strips above the roof and flag to create two bursts of fireworks, gently curving the pieces and trimming them as needed. When you are happy with the placement, fuse them in place. Thread your machine with the silver metallic thread and stitch the pieces in place. We used a machine overlock stitch. Set the stitch width so that it is as wide as the wool strip. You could sew a blanket stitch on both edges of the strips if you prefer.

Overlock stitch

Adding the Borders

①　Stitch red-and-cream 1" x 14½" strips to the top and bottom of the quilt top. Sew the 1" x 39½" red-and-cream strips to the sides of the quilt top.

②　Stitch the 2" x 39½" navy plaid strips to the sides of the quilt top. Sew the 2" red-and-cream squares to the ends of the two 2" x 15½" navy plaid strips. Add the pieced border strips to the top and bottom of the quilt top.

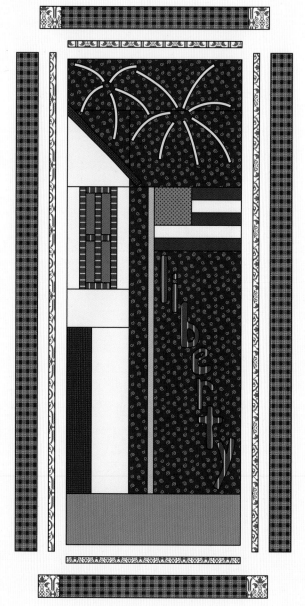

Banner assembly

Finishing

Refer to "Quilting and Binding" on page 7 to layer the quilt top, batting, and backing. Quilt as desired. Bind the quilt with the 1½" navy blue 2 strips.

Roof

Harvest Door Banner

The rich colors in this door banner will greet your autumn guests with welcoming warmth. The teal blue sky gives you a sense of a cool nip in the air, while the orange and gold hues take off the chill, just as the sun does to brisk fall days.

~Tammy

Quilted by Sue Urich

Finished banner size: 18" x 42"

Materials

Yardage is based on 42"-wide fabric.

⅝ yard of red-and-blue plaid for letter appliqués, border, and binding

½ yard of teal blue print for background

¼ yard of tan print for house

¼ yard of green striped fabric for ground

¼ yard of orange mottled print for pumpkin

⅛ yard of red print for door and window trim

⅛ yard of green print for sunflower stem

Scrap of gold print, at least 3¾" x 5", for window

Scrap of gold plaid, at least 6" x 9", for sunflower

Scrap of green print, at least 5" x 7", for leaves

Scrap of black-and-gold print, at least 3" x 5", for sunflower center

Scrap of brown-and-green print, at least 4" x 6", for pumpkin stem

Scrap of brown checked fabric, at least 1" x 10", for roof appliqué

Scraps of 16 assorted green, blue, gold, and red prints, at least 3" square, for border half-square-triangle units

1½ yards of fabric for backing

24" x 48" piece of batting

1 yard of paper-backed fusible web

Cutting

The appliqué patterns are found on pages 62 and 63. For more information on cutting pieces for fusible appliqué, refer to "Fusible Appliqué" on page 6.

From the teal blue print, cut:
- 1 rectangle, 9½" x 13½"
- 1 rectangle, 5½" x 7½"
- 1 square, 5½" x 5½"
- 1 rectangle, 4½" x 14½"
- 1 rectangle, 2½" x 17½"
- 1 rectangle, 1½" x 17½"
- 1 rectangle, 1½" x 10½"
- 4 squares, 1½" x 1½"

From the tan print, cut:
- 1 rectangle, 5½" x 6½"
- 1 rectangle, 3½" x 13½"
- 1 rectangle, 3½" x 5½"
- 2 rectangles, 1½" x 8½"

From the gold print, cut:
- 4 rectangles, 1¼" x 3¾"

From the red print, cut:
- 1 rectangle, 2½" x 13½"
- 2 rectangles, 1" x 8½"
- 1 rectangle, 1" x 7½"
- 2 rectangles, 1" x 2½"
- 2 rectangles, 1" x 1¼"

From the orange mottled print, cut:
• 1 rectangle, 4½" x 10½"

From the green print for stem, cut:
• 1 rectangle, 1½" x 17½"

From the green striped fabric, cut:
• 1 rectangle, 4½" x 14½"

From the brown checked scrap, cut:
• 1 roof appliqué shape

From the brown-and-green print, cut:
• 1 pumpkin stem appliqué shape

From the green print for leaves, cut:
• 1 leaf appliqué shape
• 1 reverse leaf appliqué shape

From the gold plaid scrap, cut:
• 1 outer sunflower appliqué shape

From the black-and-gold print, cut:
• 1 sunflower center appliqué shape

From the red-and-blue plaid, cut:
• 8 squares, 2⅞" x 2⅞"; cut each square once diagonally to yield 16 triangles
• 2 rectangles, 2½" x 17½"
• 2 rectangles, 2½" x 13½"
• 2 rectangles, 2½" x 10½"
• 4 binding strips, 1½" x 42"
• 1 *each* of appliqué shapes H, A, R, V, E, S, and T

From the assorted green, blue, gold, and red prints, cut a *total* of:
• 16 squares, 2⅞" x 2⅞"; cut each square once diagonally to yield 32 triangles (you will use 16)

Constructing the House Section

① Refer to "Folded Corners" on page 5 to fold the teal blue 5½" square in half diagonally and place it on the tan print 5½" x 6½" rectangle, with the marked line in the direction shown and the top and side edges aligned. Stitch on the marked line, trim ¼" from the stitching, and press the

resulting triangle over the seam to complete the roof unit.

② Sew gold print 1¼" x 3¾" rectangles to the long edges of a red print 1" x 1¼" rectangle. Repeat to make a total of two windowpane units.

Make 2.

③ Stitch a windowpane unit to each side of the red print 1" x 7½" rectangle. Add red print 1" x 2½" rectangles to the top and bottom of this unit.

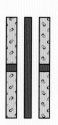

④ Sew a red print 1" x 8½" rectangle to each side of the unit from step 3, and then add a tan print 1½" x 8½" rectangle to each side. Join the tan print 3½" x 5½" rectangle to the bottom to complete the window unit.

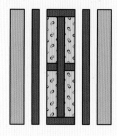 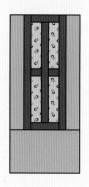

⑤ Sew the red print 2½" x 13½" rectangle and the tan print 3½" x 13½" rectangle together. Add this unit to the bottom of the window unit. Sew the roof unit to the top of the window unit.

② Sew the teal blue 1½" x 10½" rectangle to the left side of the pumpkin unit. Add the teal blue 5½" x 7½" rectangle to the top of the unit.

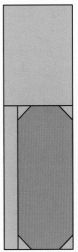

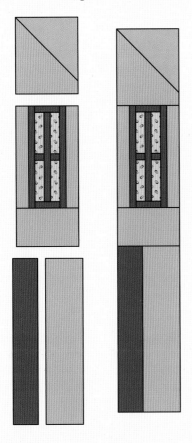

Constructing the Pumpkin and Sunflower Section

① Refer to "Folded Corners" to fold the four teal blue 1½" squares in half diagonally. Place a square on each corner of the orange mottled rectangle, with the marked lines in the directions shown. Stitch on the marked lines, trim ¼" from the stitching, and press the resulting triangles over the seams to make the pumpkin unit.

③ Sew the teal blue 1½" x 17½" rectangle, the green print 1½" x 17½" rectangle, and the teal blue 2½" x 17½" rectangle together side by side. Add this unit to the right edge of the pumpkin unit. Join the teal blue 9½" x 13½" rectangle to the top.

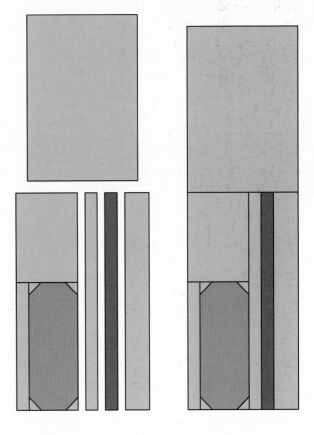

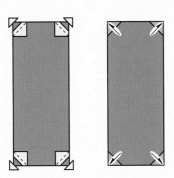

Joining the Sections

Sew the pumpkin and sunflower section to the right edge of the house section. Add the teal blue 4½" x 14½" rectangle to the top of the joined sections and the green striped 4½" x 14½" rectangle to the bottom.

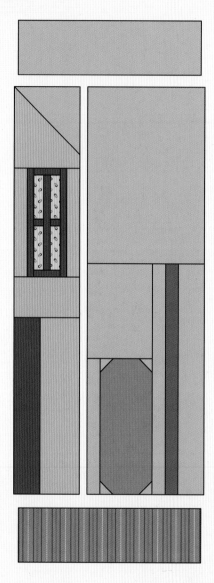

Appliquéing

Refer to "Fusible Appliqué" on page 6 and the photo on page 57 to position each appliqué shape on the quilt top as indicated below. When you are happy with the placement, fuse the shapes in place. Machine blanket stitch around each appliqué with matching thread.

① Appliqué the roof shape to the diagonal seam at the top of the house section.

② Appliqué the pumpkin stem to the top of the pumpkin.

③ Appliqué the sunflower leaves, and then the outer sunflower to the green print stem. Appliqué the sunflower center to the sunflower head.

④ Appliqué the letters to the area above the house and pumpkin and sunflower sections.

Adding the Border

① Sew each red-and-blue plaid triangle to an assorted green, blue, gold, or red triangle to make 16 half-square-triangle units.

Make 16.

② Sew the half-square-triangle units together as shown to make border units A, B, and C.

Unit A.   Unit B.
Make 2.   Make 2.

Unit C.
Make 2.

③ Refer to the quilt assembly diagram to stitch a red-and-blue plaid 2½" x 10½" rectangle and a B border unit together. Repeat to make a total of two strips. Stitch these strips to the top and bottom of the quilt top. Stitch together a red-and-blue plaid 2½" x 13½" rectangle, an A border unit, a C border unit, and a red-and-blue plaid 2½" x 17½" rectangle. Repeat to make a total of two strips. Sew these units to the sides of the quilt top.

Finishing

Refer to "Quilting and Binding" on page 7 to layer the quilt top, batting, and backing. Quilt as desired. Bind the quilt with the red-and-blue plaid 1½" strips.

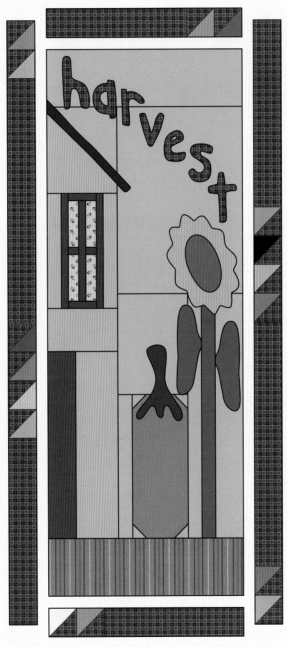

Banner assembly

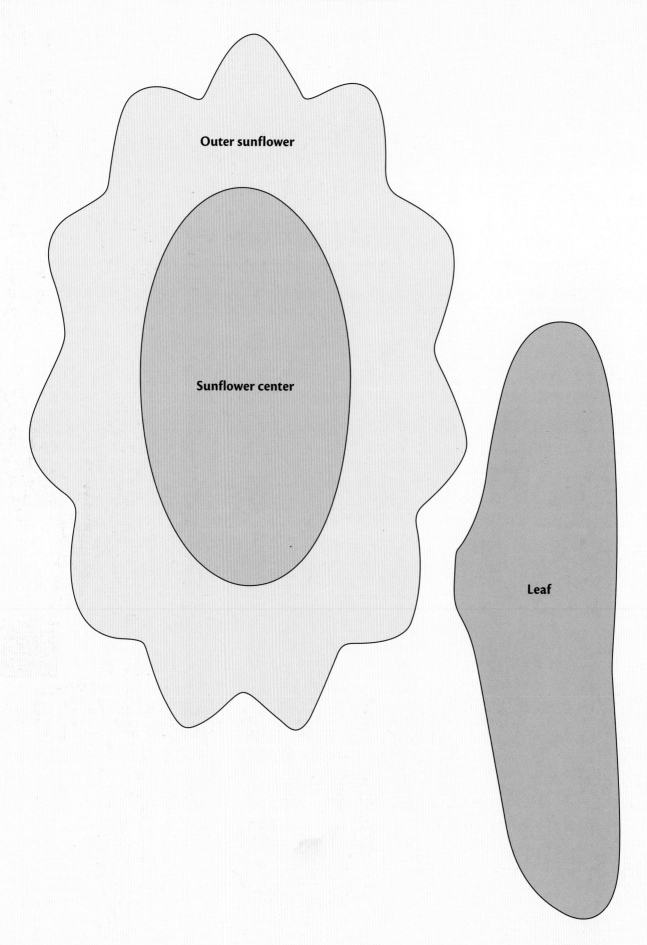

Outer sunflower

Sunflower center

Leaf

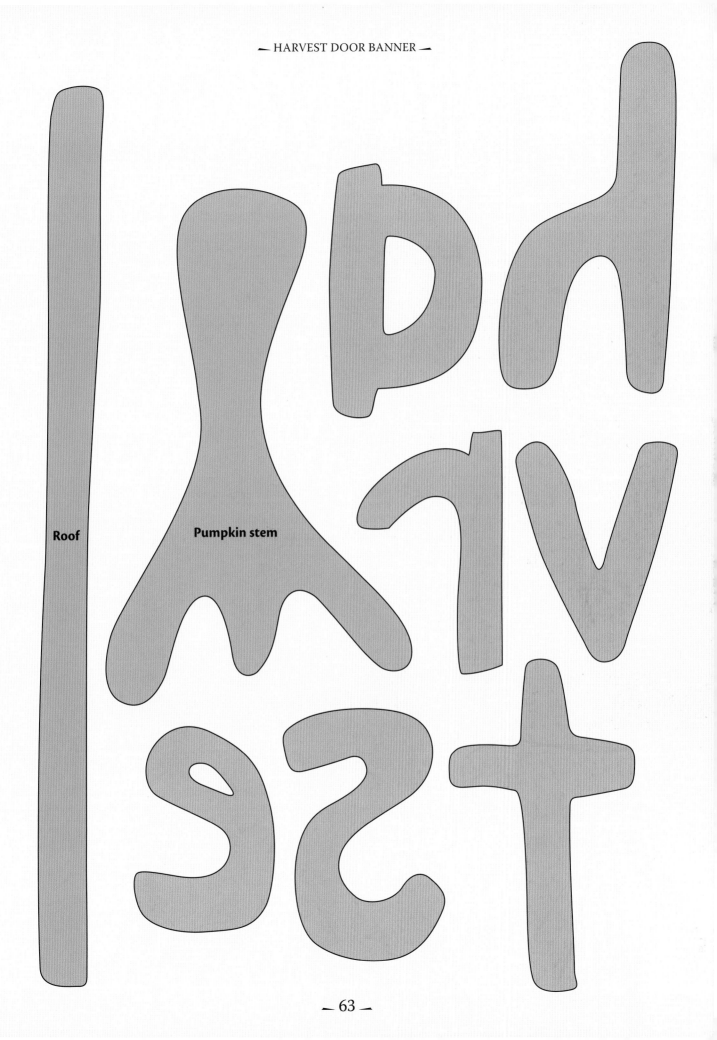

Roof

Pumpkin stem

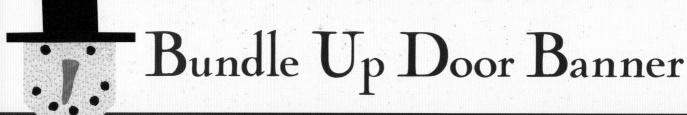

Bundle Up Door Banner

Brrrr—it's cold outside, but this door banner will usher friends and family into your home with a warm welcome. The creamy whites and icy blues might give you a chill, but a cup of hot cocoa will take care of that.

~Tammy

Quilted by Sue Urich

Finished banner size: 18" x 42"

Materials

Yardage is based on 42"-wide fabric.

⅝ yard of black-and-blue striped fabric for letter appliqués, border, and binding

⅓ yard of light blue print for background

⅓ yard of off-white print for snowman

¼ yard of ecru plaid for house

¼ yard of cream print for ground

¼ yard of blue print for border

⅛ yard of brown checked fabric for door and window trim

⅛ yard of cream solid for snowflake appliqués

⅛ yard of brown print for roof and arm appliqués

Scrap of black solid, at least 5" x 8", for hat, eye, and mouth appliqués

Scrap of gold print, at least 3¾" x 5", for windows

Scrap of orange fabric, at least 2" x 3", for nose appliqué

1½ yards of fabric for backing

24" x 48" piece of batting

1 yard of paper-backed fusible web

4 large assorted buttons

Cutting

The appliqué patterns are found on pages 70 and 71. For more information on cutting pieces for fusible appliqué, refer to "Fusible Appliqué" on page 6.

From the light blue print, cut:
• 1 rectangle, 6½" x 9½"
• 1 square, 5½" x 5½"
• 1 rectangle, 4½" x 14½"
• 2 rectangles, 2½" x 12½"
• 2 rectangles, 2½" x 3½"
• 2 squares, 2½" x 2½"
• 2 rectangles, 1½" x 9½"
• 8 squares, 1½" x 1½"
• 2 rectangles, 1" x 2½"

From the ecru plaid, cut:
• 1 rectangle, 5½" x 6½"
• 1 rectangle, 3½" x 13½"
• 1 rectangle, 3½" x 5½"
• 2 rectangles, 1½" x 8½"

From the gold print, cut:
• 4 rectangles, 1¼" x 3¾"

From the brown checked fabric, cut:
• 1 rectangle, 2½" x 13½"
• 2 rectangles, 1" x 8½"
• 1 rectangle, 1" x 7½"
• 2 rectangles, 1" x 2½"
• 2 rectangles, 1" x 1¼"

From the off-white print, cut:
- 1 rectangle, 7½" x 9½"
- 1 rectangle, 5½" x 8½"
- 1 rectangle, 4½" x 5½"

From the black solid, cut:
- 1 square, 3½" x 3½"
- 2 rectangles, 1" x 2½"
- 7 eye/mouth appliqué shapes

From the cream print, cut:
- 1 rectangle, 4½" x 14½"

From the brown print, cut:
- 1 roof appliqué shape
- 2 arm appliqué shapes

From the orange scrap, cut:
- 1 nose appliqué shape

From the cream solid, cut:
- 3 snowflake appliqué shapes

From the black-and-blue striped fabric, cut:
- 8 rectangles, 2½" x 7½"
- 4 binding strips, 1½" x 42"
- 1 *each* of appliqué shapes B, N, D, L, E, and P
- 2 U appliqué shapes
- 1 exclamation point appliqué shape

From the blue print, cut:
- 8 rectangles, 2½" x 7½"

Constructing the House Section

① Refer to "Folded Corners" on page 5 to fold the light blue 5½" square in half diagonally and place it on the ecru plaid 5½" x 6½" rectangle, with the marked line in the direction shown and the top and side edges aligned. Stitch on the marked line, trim ¼" from the stitching, and press the resulting triangle over the seam to complete the roof unit.

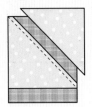

② Sew gold print 1¼" x 3¾" rectangles to the long edges of a brown checked 1" x 1¼" rectangle. Repeat to make a total of two windowpane units.

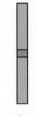

Make 2.

③ Stitch a windowpane unit to each side of the brown checked 1" x 7½" rectangle. Add brown checked 1" x 2½" rectangles to the top and bottom of this unit.

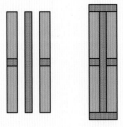

④ Sew a brown checked 1" x 8½" rectangle to each side of the unit from step 3, and then add an ecru plaid 1½" x 8½" rectangle to each side. Join the ecru plaid 3½" x 5½" rectangle to the bottom to complete the window unit.

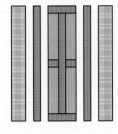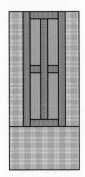

⑤ Sew the brown checked 2½" x 13½" rectangle and the ecru plaid 3½" x 13½" rectangle together. Add this unit to the bottom of the window unit. Sew the roof unit to the top of the window unit.

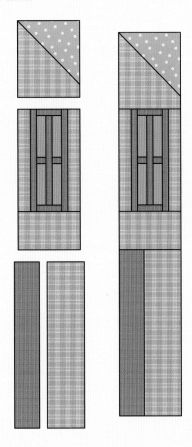

Constructing the Snowman Section

① Refer to "Folded Corners" to fold the light blue 1½" and 2½" squares in half diagonally. Place two 1½" squares on the top left and right corners of the off-white 7½" x 9½" rectangle, with the marked lines in the directions shown. Stitch on the marked line, trim ¼" from the stitching, and press the resulting triangles over the seams. Repeat on the bottom corners with the two 2½" squares.

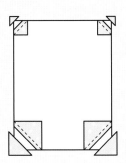

② Sew light blue 1½" x 9½" rectangles to the sides of the unit from step 1 to complete the bottom unit.

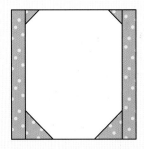

③ Place two marked light blue 1½" squares on the top corners of the off-white 5½" x 8½" rectangle. Stitch, trim, and press as before to complete the middle unit.

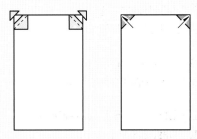

④ Repeat step 3 on the bottom corners of the off-white 4½" x 5½" rectangle to complete the top unit.

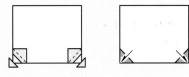

⑤ Sew the top and middle units together. Add light blue 2½" x 12½" rectangles to the sides.

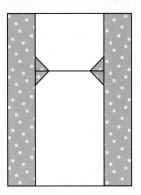

6 Add the bottom unit to the bottom of the unit from step 5.

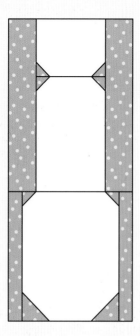

7 To make the hat unit, sew a light blue 1" x 2½" rectangle and a black 1" x 2½" rectangle together along the long edges. Repeat to make a total of two units. Add a light blue 1½" square to the end of each unit as shown.

Make 1 of each.

8 Sew light blue 2½" x 3½" rectangles to the tops of the units from step 7. Join these units to each side of the black 3½" square. Add the light blue 6½" x 9½" rectangle to the top of this unit to complete the hat unit.

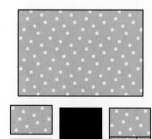

9 Sew the hat unit to the top of the unit from step 6.

Joining the Sections

Sew the snowman section to the right edge of the house section. Add the light blue 4½" x 14½" rectangle to the top of the joined sections and the cream print 4½" x 14½" rectangle to the bottom.

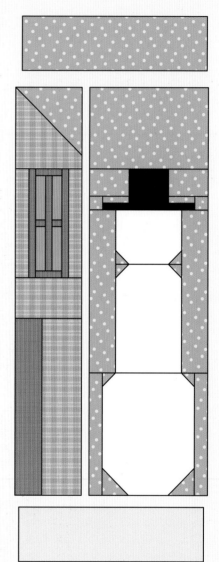

Appliquéing

Refer to "Fusible Appliqué" on page 6 and the photo on page 65 to position each appliqué shape on the quilt top as indicated below. When you are happy with the placement, fuse the shapes in place. Machine blanket stitch around each appliqué with matching thread.

1 Appliqué the roof shape to the diagonal seam at the top of the house section.

② Appliqué the letters, exclamation point, and snowflakes to the area above the roof and snowman sections.

③ Appliqué the eyes, mouth, and nose to the snowman's face. Appliqué the arms to the snowman's middle unit.

Adding the Border

① Stitch together a black-and-blue striped and a blue print 2½" x 7½" rectangle along the short ends. Repeat to make a total of two units. Refer to the assembly diagram to stitch these units to the top and bottom of the quilt top.

② Alternately stitch together three black-and-blue striped and three blue print rectangles. Repeat to make a total of two units. Stitch these units to the sides of the quilt top.

Finishing

Refer to "Quilting and Binding" on page 7 to layer the quilt top, batting, and backing. Quilt as desired. Bind the quilt with the black-and-blue striped 1½" strips. Sew the four buttons down the center of the snowman's body.

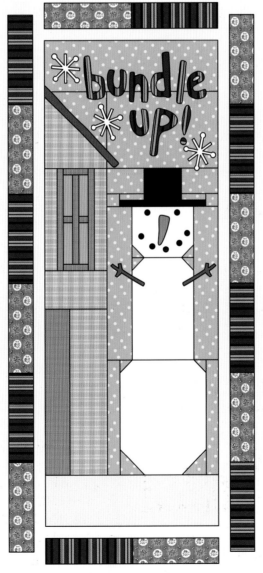

Banner assembly

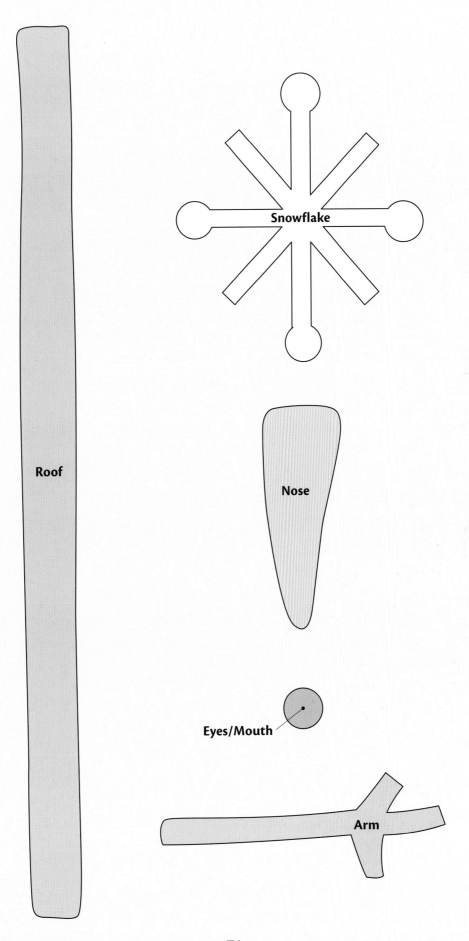

Roof

Snowflake

Nose

Eyes/Mouth

Arm

Pink Posies

Isn't there something special about a collection of antique buttons? Here, an assortment of simple, small white buttons embellish this table mat. A touch of rickrack adds to the vintage charm.

~Avis

Finished table-runner size: 13" x 25"

Materials

Felted wool is wool that has been washed and dried by machine to shrink the fibers and prevent raveling. If you are purchasing unfelted wool off the bolt, you will need to purchase extra yardage to allow for shrinkage. To felt wool, machine wash it in warm water and dry it on a medium setting in your dryer.

13" x 25" rectangle of off-white felted wool for foundation

10" x 25" rectangle of off-white houndstooth checked felted wool for tongues

6" x 18" rectangle of rose felted wool for outer flowers

4" x 12" rectangle of soft pink felted wool for flower centers

2" x 12" rectangle of green felted wool for leaves

¼ yard of 42"-wide cotton fabric for binding

½ yard of 42"-wide cotton fabric for backing

2 yards of tan medium rickrack

1 yard of paper-backed fusible web

84 *total* off-white and white buttons, ¼" to ⅝" diameter

Chalk marker

Cutting

The appliqué patterns are found on page 75; only the flower pieces will be cut here. For more information on cutting pieces for fusible appliqué, refer to "Fusible Applique" on page 6.

From the rose felted wool, cut:
• 3 outer flower appliqué shapes

From the soft pink felted wool, cut:
• 3 flower center appliqué shapes

From the green felted wool, cut:
• 6 leaf appliqué shapes

From the fabric for backing, cut:
• 1 rectangle, 13" x 25"

From the fabric for binding, cut:
• 2 strips, 1½" x 42"

Constructing the Table-Runner Top

1. Make sure that the off-white foundation piece measures 13" x 25". Using a chalk marker, draw a line 2½" in from the outer edges.

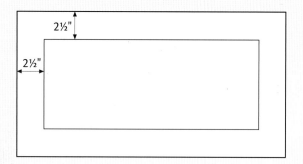

2. Trace the tongue pattern on page 75 onto the paper side of the fusible web. When tracing, do not make individual tongues, but rather trace in one continuous strip. For the ends, trace two units with four tongues each; for the sides, trace two units with ten tongues each. Roughly cut around the units.

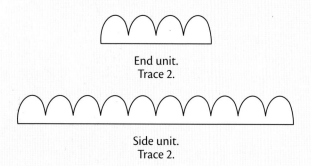

End unit.
Trace 2.

Side unit.
Trace 2.

3. Refer to "Fusible Appliqué" on page 6 to fuse the tongue units to the wrong side of the off-white houndstooth checked felted wool piece and cut them out. Position the tongue units on the foundation piece, having the straight edges even with the drawn lines; fuse them in place. Stitch around each tongue with a blanket stitch and matching thread.

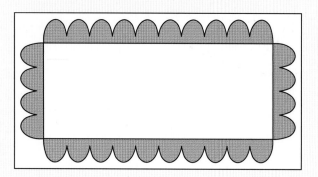

4. Cut two pieces of rickrack 22" long and two pieces 10" long. Turn under 1" on the ends of each piece. Pin the long pieces of rickrack in place along the long straight edges of each tongue side unit, and then pin the short rickrack pieces to the ends. The rickrack can be attached one of two ways: machine straight stitch down the center of the rickrack, or attach the rickrack while sewing on the inner row of buttons (see step 5). Securing the rickrack with the button will leave the rickrack loose between the buttons, which was done in the original.

5. Refer to the photo on page 73 to sew on the buttons. Align the inner row of buttons on top of the rickrack so they are centered on the long edge of the tongue. We used our sewing machine to attach the buttons. Please refer to your sewing machine manual for instructions, or sew the buttons on by hand. Sew two additional buttons to each tongue, aligning them with the first button.

Appliquéing the Flowers

Refer to "Fusible Appliqué" on page 6 and the photo on page 73 to position the outer flowers on the table-runner top. Place a flower center on each outer flower, and then tuck the straight edge of two leaves under each outer flower. When you are happy with the placement, fuse the shapes in place. Machine blanket stitch around each appliqué with matching thread.

Finishing

Layer the table-runner top and the backing rectangle wrong sides together. Refer to "Quilting and Binding" on page 7 to bind the runner with the 1½" binding strips.

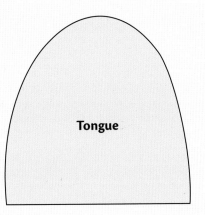

Tongue

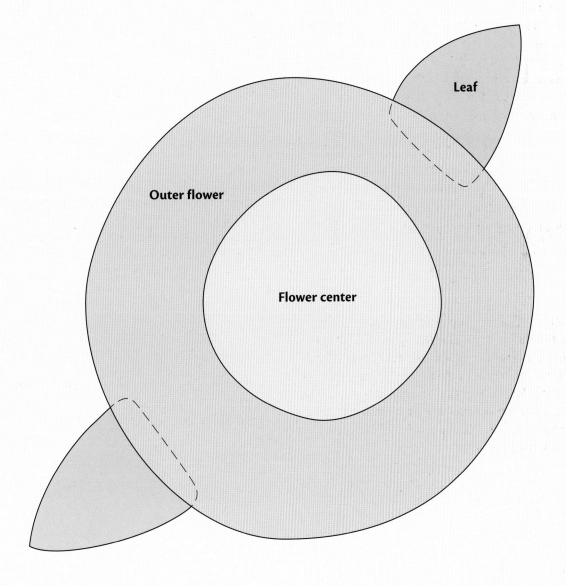

Leaf

Outer flower

Flower center

Posies Sachet

With its divine combination of vintage rickrack and buttons,
this lavender-filled sachet will be a welcome addition to any drawer.

~Avis

Materials

Felted wool is wool that has been washed and dried by machine to shrink the fibers and prevent raveling. If you are purchasing unfelted wool off the bolt, you will need to purchase extra yardage to allow for shrinkage. To felt wool, machine wash it in warm water and dry it on a medium setting in your dryer.

9" x 18" rectangle of off-white felted wool

6" x 6" square of rose felted wool

4" x 4" square of soft pink felted wool

⅔ yard of crocheted button trim

⅔ yard of ecru medium rickrack

2 assorted buttons, 1" to 1¼" diameter

¼ yard of paper-backed fusible web

1½ to 2 cups of dried lavender buds or fiberfill

Tapestry needle

Carpet thread to match buttons

Cutting

The appliqué patterns are found on page 79. For more information on cutting pieces for fusible appliqué, refer to "Fusible Appliqué" on page 6. The cutting pattern for the foundation (A) is found on page 78.

From the off-white wool, cut:
• 2 using pattern A

From the rose wool, cut:
• 1 large circle appliqué shape

From the soft pink wool, cut:
• 1 small circle appliqué shape

Construction

① Refer to "Fusible Appliqué" on page 6 to center the rose circle on the right side of one of the off-white circles and fuse it in place. Machine blanket stitch around the rose circle with matching thread. In the same manner, fuse the pink circle to the rose circle and stitch it in place with matching thread.

② Lay the appliquéd circle and the remaining off white circle right sides together. Using a ¼" seam allowance, stitch around the circle, leaving an opening for turning as indicated on the pattern. Turn the piece right side out. Stuff the circle firmly with lavender or fiberfill. Slip-stitch the opening closed.

Finished sachet size: 6" diameter

Embellishing

1. Align the edge of the crocheted button trim with the sachet seam. Hand stitch the trim to the sachet using small stitches, turning the raw ends of the trim under.

2. Lay the rickrack over the upper edge of the crochet trim. Fold the raw ends of the rickrack under and stitch it in place by hand, using small stitches to tack the trim in place.

3. Thread the tapestry needle with a length of carpet thread. Center the buttons on the top and bottom of the sachet. Insert the needle through the top button, into the sachet, and then through the bottom button. Pull the thread tight to give a slight indentation. Continue going back and forth through the sachet and buttons to secure and lock the buttons in place.

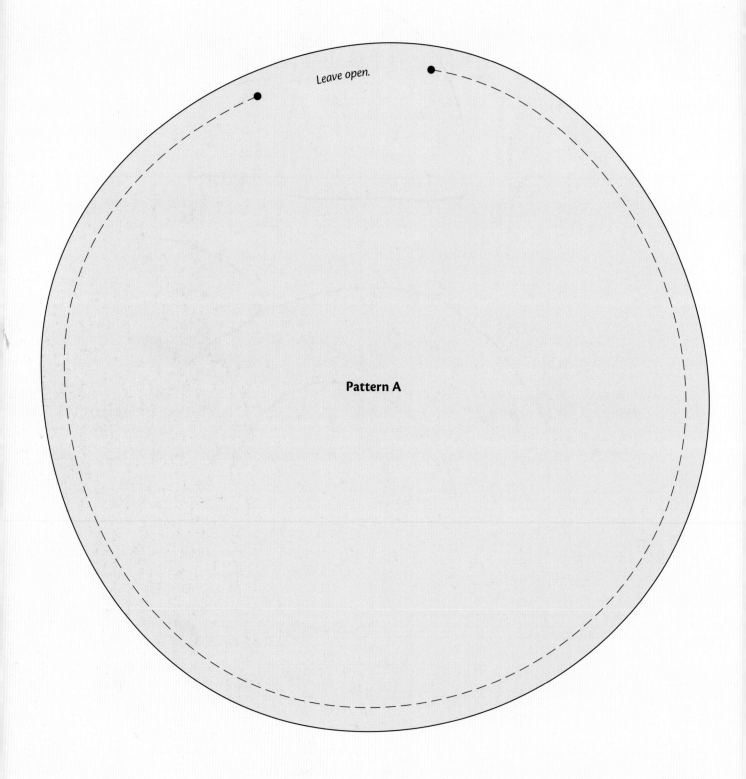

Leave open.

Pattern A

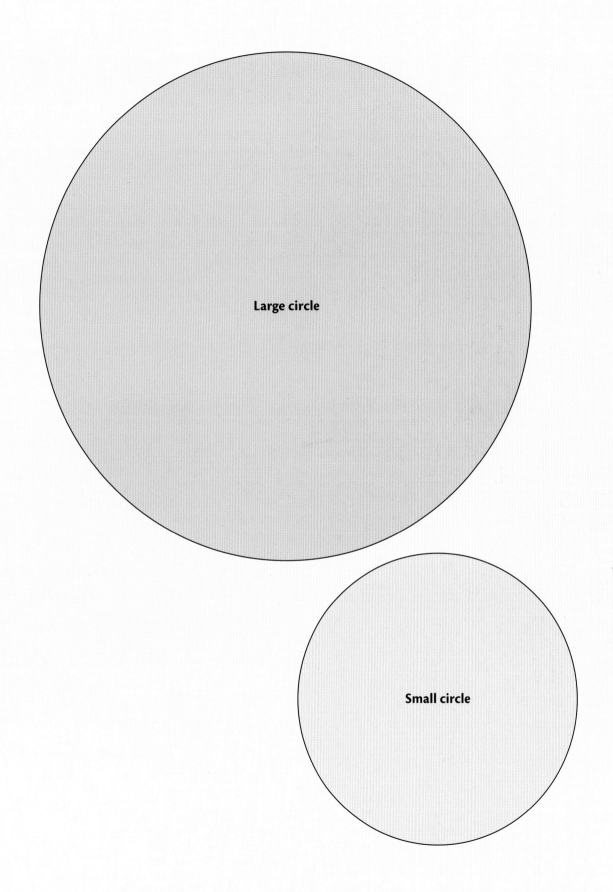

Large circle

Small circle

About the Authors

Tammy and Avis have self-published 12 quilt books and over 100 patterns, including their popular Button Up series and Simple Woolens series. They have also designed five lines of fabric. They are well known for their primitive, whimsical designs, and love to combine many elements in their quilt designs, including appliqué, patchwork, and traditional quilting fabrics as well as wool, rickrack, buttons, and more to add to the overall charm. For more information about their books and patterns, visit www.joinedatthehip.com.

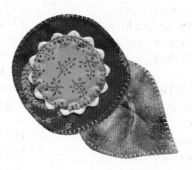